The Creative Process In The Individual And The Dore Lectures

Judge Thomas Troward

ISBN 1425454232

Discover Thousands

Of Scarce

And

Hard-To-Find

Book Reprints!

Visit Out Website At:

www.kessinger.net

The Edinburgh Lecture Series

THE CREATIVE PROCESS IN THE INDIVIDUAL

BY

T. TROWARD

(Late Divisional Judge, Punjab. Honorary member of the Medico-Legal Society of New York)

Author of the "Edinburgh Lectures on Mental Science," etc.

NEW AND ENLARGED EDITION

NEW YORK

ROBERT M. McBRIDE & COMPANY

1920.

Third Printing
May, 1917
Fourth Printing
June, 1919
Fifth Printing
December, 1920

PRINTED IN THE UNITED STATES OF AMERICA

Published June, 1915

Kessinger Publishing's Rare Reprints
Thousands of Scarce and Hard-to-Find Books!

- Americana
- Ancient Mysteries
- Animals
- Anthropology
- Architecture
- Arts
- Astrology
- Bibliographies
- Biographies & Memoirs
- Body, Mind & Spirit
- Business & Investing
- Children & Young Adult
- Collectibles
- Comparative Religions
- Crafts & Hobbies
- Earth Sciences
- Education
- Ephemera
- Fiction

- Folklore
- Geography
- Health & Diet
- History
- Hobbies & Leisure
- Humor
- Illustrated Books
- Language & Culture
- Law
- Life Sciences
- Literature
- Medicine & Pharmacy
- Metaphysical
- Music
- Mystery & Crime
- Mythology
- Natural History
- Outdoor & Nature
- Philosophy

- Poetry
- Political Science
- Science
- Psychiatry & Psychology
- Reference
- Religion & Spiritualism
- Rhetoric
- Sacred Books
- Science Fiction
- Science & Technology
- Self-Help
- Social Sciences
- Symbolism
- Theatre & Drama
- Theology
- Travel & Explorations
- War & Military
- Women
- Yoga

We kindly invite you to view our extensive catalog list at:
http://www.kessinger.net

THE author here explains scientifically the sequence of creative action, from the first beginnings of life through the development of the race to the need of the present day—the perfect realization of the divine right of creation. The knowledge of oneself—made in the likeness of the great creative Power and necessarily sharing in that power to create what is good—will open up a wonderful vista of possibilities to all who follow unerringly the law of their own being. If we knowingly and willingly co-operate with this law, our outlook upon life broadens to great interests and to certainty in our own efforts toward accomplishing whatever end we desire —a wonderful promise to the faithful student.

FOREWORD

In the present volume I have endeavored to set before the reader the conception of a sequence of creative action commencing with the formation of the globe and culminating in a vista of infinite possibilities attainable by every one who follows up the right line for their unfoldment.

I have endeavored to show that, starting with certain incontrovertible scientific facts, all these things logically follow, and that therefore, however far these speculations may carry us beyond our past experience, they nowhere break the thread of an intelligible connection of cause and effect.

I do not, however, offer the suggestions here put forward in any other light than that of purely speculative reasoning; nevertheless, no advance in any direction can be made except by speculative reasoning going back to the first principles of things which we do know and thence deducing the conditions under which the same principles might be carried further and made to produce results hitherto unknown. It is to this method of thought that we owe all the advantages of civilization from matches and post-offices to motor-cars and aeroplanes, and we may therefore be encouraged to hope such speculations as the present may not be without their ultimate value. Relying on the maxim that Principle is not bound by Precedent we should not limit our expectations of the future; and if our speculations lead us to the conclusion that we have reached a point where we are not only able, but also *required,* by the law of our own being, to take a more active part in our personal evolution than heretofore, this discovery will afford us a new outlook upon life and widen our horizon with fresh interests and brightening hopes.

If the thoughts here suggested should help any reader to clear some mental obstacles from his path the writer will feel that he has not written to no purpose. Only each reader must think out these suggestions for himself. No writer or lecturer can convey an idea *into* the minds of his audience. He can only put it before them, and what they will make of it depends entirely upon themselves — assimilation is a process which no one can carry out for us.

To the kindness of my readers on both sides of the Atlantic, and in Australia and New Zealand, I commend this little volume, not, indeed, without a deep sense of its many short-comings, but at the same time encouraged by the generous indulgence extended to my previous books.

T.T.

June, 1910.

CONTENTS

THE CREATIVE PROCESS IN
THE INDIVIDUAL

I say no man has ever yet been half devout enough,
None has ever yet adored or worship'd half enough,
None has begun to think how divine he himself is, and
how certain the future is.
I say that the real and permanent grandeur of these States
must be their religion,
Otherwise there is no real and permanent grandeur.
—WALT WHITMAN.

THE CREATIVE PROCESS IN THE INDIVIDUAL

CHAPTER I

THE STARTING-POINT

IT is an old saying that "Order is Heaven's First Law," and like many other old sayings it contains a much deeper philosophy than appears immediately on the surface. Getting things into a better order is the great secret of progress, and we are now able to fly through the air, not because the laws of Nature have altered, but because we have learnt to arrange things in the right order to produce this result — the things themselves had existed from the beginning of the world, but what was wanting was the introduction of a Personal Factor which, by an intelligent perception of the possibilities contained in the laws of Nature, should be able to bring into working reality ideas which previous generations would

I

have laughed at as the absurd fancies of an unbalanced mind. The lesson to be learnt from the practical aviation of the present day is that of the triumph of principle over precedent, of the working out of an *idea* to its logical conclusions in spite of the accumulated testimony of all past experience to the contrary; and with such a notable example before us can we say that it is futile to enquire whether by the same method we may not unlock still more important secrets and gain some knowledge of the unseen causes which are at the back of external and visible conditions, and then by bringing these unseen causes into a better order make practical working realities of possibilities which at present seem but fantastic dreams? It is at least worth while taking a preliminary canter over the course, and this is all that this little volume professes to attempt; yet this may be sufficient to show the lay of the ground.

Now the first thing in any investigation is to have some idea of what you are looking for — to have at least some notion of the general direction in which to go — just as you would not go up a tree to find fish though you would for birds' eggs. Well, the general direction in which we all want to go is that of getting more out of Life than we have ever got out of it — we want to be more alive in ourselves and to get all sorts of improved conditions in our environment. However happily any of us may be circumstanced we can all conceive something still better, or at any rate we should like to make our present good permanent; and since we shall find as our studies advance that the prospect of increasing possibilities keeps opening out more and more widely before us, we may say that what we are in search of is the secret of getting more out of Life in a continually progressive degree. This means that what we are looking for is something personal, and that it is to be obtained by producing conditions which do not yet exist; in other words it is nothing less than the exercise of a certain creative power in the sphere of our own particular world. So, then, what we want is to introduce our own Personal Factor into the realm of unseen causes. This is a big thing, and if it is possible at all it must be by some sequence of cause and effect, and this sequence it is our object to discover. The law of Cause and Effect is one we can never get away from, but by carefully following it up we may find that it will lead us further than we had anticipated.

Now, the first thing to observe is that if *we* can succeed in finding out such a sequence of cause and effect as the one we are in search of, somebody else may find out the same creative secret also; and then, by the hypothesis of the case, we should both be armed with an infallible power, and if we wanted to employ this power against each other we should be landed in the "impasse" of a conflict between two powers each of which was irresistible. Consequently it follows that the first principle of this power must be Harmony. It cannot be antagonizing itself from different centers — in other words its operation in a simultaneous order at every point is the first necessity of its being. What we are in search of, then, is a sequence of cause and effect so universal in its nature as to include harmoniously all possible variations of individual expression. This primary necessity of the Law for which we are seeking should be carefully borne in mind, for it is obvious that any sequence which transgresses this primary essential must be contrary to the very nature of the Law itself, and consequently cannot be conducting us to the exercise of true creative power.

What we are seeking, therefore, is to discover how to arrange things in such an order as to set in motion a train of causation that will harmonize our own conditions without antagonizing the exercise of a like power by others. This therefore means that all individual exercise of this power is the particular application of a universal power which itself operates creatively on its own account independently of these individual applications; and the harmony between the various individual applications is brought about by all the individuals bringing their own particular action into line with this independent creative action of the original power. It is in fact another application of Euclid's axiom that things which are equal to the same thing are equal to one another; so that though I may not know for what purpose some one may be using this creative power in Pekin, I do know that if he and I both realize its true nature we cannot by any possibility be working in opposition to one another. For these reasons, having now some general idea of what it is we are in search of, we may commence our investigation by considering this common factor which must be at the back of all individual exercise of creative power, that is to say, the Generic working of the Universal Creative Principle.

That such a Universal Creative Principle is at work we at once realize from the existence of the world around us with all its inhabitants, and the inter-relation of all parts of the cosmic system shows its underlying Unity — thus the animal kingdom depends on the vegetable, the vegetable kingdom on the mineral, the mineral or globe of the earth on its relation to the rest of the solar system, and possibly our solar system is related by a similar law to the distribution of other suns with their attendant planets throughout space. Our first glance therefore shows us that the All-originating Power must be in essence Unity and in manifestation Multiplicity, and that it manifests as Life and Beauty through the unerring adaptation of means to ends — that is so far as its cosmic manifestation of ends goes: what we want to do is to carry this manifestation still further by operation from an individual standpoint. To do this is precisely our place in the Order of Creation, but we must defer the question why we hold this place till later on.

One of the earliest discoveries we all make is the existence of Matter. The bruised shins of our childhood convince us of its solidity, so now comes the question, Why does Matter exist? The answer is that if the form were not expressed in solid substance, things would be perpetually flowing into each other so that no identity could be maintained for a single moment. To this it might be replied that a condition of matter is conceivable in which, though in itself a plastic substance, in a fluent state, it might yet by the operation of will be held in any particular forms desired. The idea of such a condition of matter is no doubt conceivable, and when the fluent matter was thus held in particular forms you would have concrete matter just as we know it now, only with this difference, that it would return to its fluent state as soon as the supporting will was withdrawn. Now, as we shall see later on, this is precisely what matter really is, only the will which holds it together in concrete form is not individual but cosmic.

In itself the Essence of Matter is precisely the fluent substance we have imagined, and as we shall see later on the knowledge of this fact, when realized in its proper order, is the basis of the legitimate control of mind over matter. But a world in which every individual possessed the power of concreting or fluxing matter at his own sweet will irrespective of any universal coordinating principle is altogether inconceivable — the conflict of wills would prevent such a world remaining in existence. On the other hand if we conceive of a number of individuals each possessing this power and all employing it on the lines of a common cosmic unity, then the result would be precisely the same stable condition of matter with which we are familiar — this would be a necessity of fact for the masses who did not possess this power, and a necessity of principle for the few who did. So under these circumstances the same stable conditions of Nature would prevail as at present, varied only when the initiated ones perceived that the order of evolution would be furthered, and not hindered, by calling into action the higher laws. Such occasions would be of rare occurrence, and then the departure from the ordinary law would be regarded by the multitude as a miracle. Also we may be quite sure that no one who had attained this knowledge in the

legitimate order would ever perform a
" miracle " for his own personal aggrandize-
ment or for the purpose of merely astonishing
the beholders — to do so would be contrary to
the first principle of the higher teaching which
is that of profound reverence for the Unity of
the All-originating Principle. The conception,
therefore, of such a power over matter being
possessed by certain individuals is in no way
opposed to our ordinary recognition of concrete matter, and so we need not at present
trouble ourselves to consider these exceptions.

Another theory is that matter has no existence at all but is merely an illusion projected
by our own minds. If so, then how is it that
we all project identically similar images? On
the supposition that each mind is independently
projecting its own conception of matter a lady
who goes to be fitted might be seen by her
dressmaker as a cow. Generations of people
have seen the Great Pyramid on the same spot;
but on the supposition that each individual is
projecting his own material world in entire
independence of all other individuals there is
no reason why any two persons should ever
see the same thing in the same place. On the
supposition of such an independent action by

each separate mind, without any common factor binding them all to one particular mode of recognition, no intercourse between individuals would be possible — then, without the consciousness of relation to other individuals the consciousness of our own individuality would be lost, and so we should cease to have any conscious existence at all. If on the other hand we grant that there is, above the individual minds, a great Cosmic Mind which imposes upon them the necessity of all seeing the same image of Matter, then that image is not a projection of the individual minds but of the Cosmic Mind; and since the individual minds are themselves similar projections of the Cosmic Mind, matter is for them just as much a reality as their own existence. I doubt not that material substance is thus projected by the all-embracing Divine Mind; but so also are our own minds projected by it, and therefore the relation between them and matter is a real relation and not a merely fictitious one.

I particularly wish the student to be clear on this point, that where two factors are projected from a common source their relation to each other becomes an absolute fact in respect of the factors themselves, notwithstanding that the power of changing that relation by substituting a different projection must necessarily always continue to reside in the originating source. To take a simple arithmetical example — by my power of mental projection working through my eyes and fingers I write 4×2. Here I have established a certain numerical relation which can only produce eight as its result. Again, I have power to change the factors and write 4×3, in which case 12 is the only possible result, and so on. Working in this way calculation becomes possible. But if every time I wrote 4 that figure possessed an independent power of setting down a different number by which to multiply itself, what would be the result? The first 4 I wrote might set down 3 as its multiplier, and the next might set down 7, and so on. Or if I want to make a box of a certain size and cut lengths of plank accordingly, if each length could capriciously change its width at a moment's notice, how could I ever make the box? I myself may change the shape and size of my box by establishing new relations between the bits of wood, but for the pieces of wood themselves the proportions determined by my mind must remain fixed quantities, otherwise no construction could take place.

This is a very rough analogy, but it may be sufficient to show that for a cosmos to exist at all it is absolutely necessary that there should be a Cosmic Mind binding all individual minds to certain *generic* unities of action, and so producing all things as realities and nothing as illusion. The importance of this conclusion will become more apparent as we advance in our studies.

We have now got at some reason why concrete material form is a necessity of the Creative Process. Without it the perfect Self-recognition of Spirit from the Individual standpoint, which we shall presently find is the means by which the Creative Process is to be carried forward, would be impossible; and therefore, so far from matter being an illusion, it is the necessary channel for the self-differentiation of Spirit and its Expression in multitudinous life and beauty. Matter is thus the necessary Polar Opposite to Spirit, and when we thus recognize it in its right order we shall find that there is no antagonism between the two, but that together they constitute one harmonious whole.

CHAPTER II

THE SELF-CONTEMPLATION OF SPIRIT

IF we ask how the cosmos came into existence we shall find that ultimately we can only attribute it to the Self-Contemplation of Spirit. Let us start with the facts now known to modern physical science. All material things, including our own bodies, are composed of combinations of different chemical elements such as carbon, oxygen, nitrogen, &c. Chemistry recognizes in all about seventy of these elements each with its peculiar affinities; but the more advanced physical science of the present day finds that they are all composed of one and the same ultimate substance to which the name of Ether has been given, and that the difference between an atom of iron and an atom of oxygen results only from the difference in the number of etheric particles of which each is composed and the rate of their motion within the sphere of the atom, thus curiously coming back to the dictum of Pythagoras that the universe has its origin in Number and Motion. We may therefore say that our entire solar system together with every sort of material substance which it contains is made up of nothing but this one primary substance in various degrees of condensation.

Now the next step is to realize that this ether is everywhere. This is shown by the undulatory theory of light. Light is not a substance but is the effect produced on the eye by the impinging of the ripples of the ether upon the retina. These waves are excessively minute, ranging in length from 1-39,000th of an inch at the red end of the spectrum to 1-57,000th at the violet end. Next remember that these waves are not composed of advancing particles of the medium but pass onwards by the push which each particle in the line of motion gives to the particle next to it, and then you will see that if there were a break of one fifty-thousandth part of an inch in the connecting ether between our eye and any source of light we could not receive light from that source, for there would be nothing to continue the wave-motion across the gap. Consequently as soon as we see light from any source however distant, we know that there must be a continuous body of ether between us and it. Now astronomy shows us that we receive light from heavenly bodies so distant that, though it travels with the incredible speed of 186,000 miles per second, it takes more than two thousand years to reach us from some of them; and as such stars are in all quarters of the heavens we can only come to the conclusion that the primary substance or ether must be universally present.

This means that the raw material for the formation of solar systems is universally distributed throughout space; yet though we find that millions of suns stud the heavens, we also find vast interstellar spaces which show no sign of cosmic activity. Then something has been at work to start cosmic activity in certain areas while passing over others in which the raw material is equally available. What is this something? At first we might be inclined to attribute the development of cosmic energy to the etheric particles themselves, but a little consideration will show us that this is mathematically impossible in a medium which is equally distributed throughout space, for all its particles are in equilibrium and so no one

particle possesses *per se* a greater power of
originating motion than any other. Consequently the initial movement must be started
by something which, though it works on and
through the particles of the primary substance,
is not those particles themselves. It is this
" Something " which we mean when we speak
of " Spirit."

Then since Spirit starts the condensation of
the primary substance into concrete aggrega-
tion, and also does this in certain areas to the
exclusion of others, we cannot avoid attribut-
ing to Spirit the power of Selection and of taking an Initiative on its own account.

Here, then, we find the *initial* Polarity of
Universal Spirit and Universal Substance, each
being the complementary of the other, and out
of this relation all subsequent evolution proceeds. Being complementary means that each
supplies what is wanting in the other, and that
the two together thus make complete wholeness. Now this is just the case here. Spirit
supplies Selection and Motion. Substance
supplies something from which selection can
be made and to which Motion can be imparted;
so that it is a *sine qua non* for the Expression
of Spirit.

Then comes the question, How did the Universal Substance get there? It cannot have made itself, for its only quality is inertia, therefore it must have come from some source having power to project it by some mode of action not of a material nature. Now the only mode of action not of a material nature is Thought, and therefore to Thought we must look for the origin of Substance. This places us at a point antecedent to the existence even of primary substance, and consequently the initial action must be that of the Originating Mind upon Itself, in other words, Self-contemplation.

At this primordial stage neither Time nor Space can be recognized, for both imply measurement of successive intervals, and in the primary movement of Mind upon itself the only consciousness must be that of Present Absolute Being, because no external points exist from which to measure extension either in time or space. Hence we must eliminate the ideas of time and space from our conception of Spirit's *initial* Self-contemplation.

This being so, Spirit's primary contemplation of itself as simply Being necessarily makes its presence universal and eternal, and consequently, paradoxical as it may seem, its independence of Time and Space makes it present throughout all Time and Space. It is the old esoteric maxim that the point expands to infinitude and that infinitude is concentrated in the point. We start, then, with Spirit contemplating itself simply as Being. But to realize your being you must have consciousness, and consciousness can only come by the recognition of your relation to something else. The something else may be an external fact or a mental image; but even in the latter case to conceive the image at all you must mentally stand back from it and look at it — something like the man who was run in by the police at Gravesend for walking behind himself to see how his new coat fitted. It stands thus: if you are not conscious of something you are conscious of nothing, and if you are conscious of nothing, then you are unconscious, so that to be conscious at all you must have something to be conscious of.

This may seem like an extract from " Paddy's Philosophy," but it makes it clear that consciousness can only be attained by the recognition of something which is not the recognizing *ego* itself — in other words consciousness is the realization of some particular sort of *relation* between the cognizing subject and the cognized object; but I want to get away from academical terms into the speech of human beings, so let us take the illustration of a broom and its handle — the two together make a broom; that is one sort of relation; but take the same stick and put a rake-iron at the end of it and you have an altogether different implement. The stick remains the same, but the difference of what is put at the end of it makes the whole thing a broom or a rake. Now the thinking and feeling power is the stick, and the conception which it forms is the thing at the end of the stick, so that the quality of its consciousness will be determined by the ideas which it projects; but to be conscious at all it must project ideas of some sort.

Now of one thing we may be quite sure, that the Spirit of Life must *feel alive*. Then to feel alive it must be conscious, and to be conscious it must have something to be conscious of; therefore the contemplation of itself as standing related to something which is not its own originating self *in propria persona* is a necessity of the case; and consequently the Self-contemplation of Spirit can only proceed by its viewing itself as related to something standing out from itself, just as we must stand at a proper distance to see a picture — in fact the very word " existence " means " standing out." Thus things are called into existence or " outstandingness " by a power which itself does not stand out, and whose presence is therefore indicated by the word " subsistence."

The next thing is that since in the beginning there is nothing except Spirit, its primary feeling of aliveness must be that of being alive *all over;* and to establish such a consciousness of its own universal livingness there must be the recognition of a corresponding *relation* equally extensive in character; and the only possible correspondence to fulfil this condition is therefore that of a universally distributed and plastic medium whose particles are all in perfect equilibrium, which is exactly the description of the Primary Substance or ether. We are thus philosophically led to the conclusion that Universal Substance must be projected by Universal Spirit as a necessary consequence of Spirit's own inherent feeling of Aliveness; and in this way we find that the great Primary Polarity of Being becomes established.

From this point onward we shall find the

principle of Polarity in universal activity. It is that relation between opposites without which no external Motion would be possible, because there would be nowhere to move from, and nowhere to move to; and without which external Form would be impossible because there would be nothing to limit the diffusion of substance and bring it into shape. Polarity, or the interaction of Active and Passive, is therefore the basis of all *Evolution*.

This is a great fundamental truth when we get it in its right order; but all through the ages it has been a prolific cource of error by getting it in its wrong order. And the wrong order consists in making Polarity the originating point of the Creative Process. What this misconception leads to we shall see later on; but since it is very widely accepted under various guises even at the present day it is well to be on our guard against it. Therefore I wish the student to see clearly that there is something which comes before that Polarity which gives rise to Evolution, and that this something is the original movement of Spirit *within itself,* of which we can best get an idea by calling it Self-contemplation.

Now this may seem an extremely abstract

conception and one with which we have no
practical concern. I fancy I can hear the
reader saying " The Lord only knows how the
world started, and it is His business and not
mine," which would be perfectly true if this
originating faculty were confined to the Cosmic
Mind. But it is not, and the same action takes
place in our own minds also, only with the
difference that it is ultimately subject to that
principle of Cosmic Unity of which I have
already spoken. But, subject to that unifying
principle, this same power of origination is
in ourselves also, and our personal advance
in evolution depends on our right use of it;
and our use of it depends on our recognition
that we ourselves give rise to the particular
polarities which express themselves in our
whole world of consciousness, whether within
or without. For these reasons it is very important to realize that Evolution is not the
same as Creation. It is the unfolding of
potentialities *involved* in things already
created, but not the calling into existence of
what does not yet exist — *that* is Creation.

The order, therefore, which I wish the
student to observe is, first the Self-contemplation of Spirit producing Polarity, and next

Polarity producing Manifestation in Form — and also to realize that it is in this order his own mind operates as a subordinate center of creative energy. When the true place of Polarity is thus recognized, we shall find in it the explanation of all those relations of things which give rise to the whole world of phenomena; from which we may draw the practical inference that if we want to change the manifestation we must change the polarity, and to change the polarity we must get back to the Self-contemplation of Spirit. But in its proper place as the root-principle of all *secondary* causation, Polarity is one of those fundamental facts of which we must never lose sight. The term " Polarity " is adopted from electrical science. In the electric battery it is the connecting together of the opposite poles of zinc and copper that causes a current to flow from one to the other and so provides the energy that rings the bell. If the connection is broken there is no action. When you press the button you make the connection. The same process is repeated in respect of every sort of polarity throughout the universe. Circulation depends on polarity, and circulation is the *manifestation* of Life, which we

may therefore say depends on the principle of
polarity.   In relation to ourselves we are concerned with two great polarities, the polarity
of Soul and Body and the polarity of Soul and
Spirit; and it is in order that he may more
clearly realize their working that I want the
student to have some preliminary idea of
Polarity as a general principle.

The conception of the Creative Order may
therefore be generalized as follows.   The
Spirit wants to enjoy the reality of its own
Life — not merely to vegetate, but to enjoy
living — and therefore by Self-contemplation
it projects a polar opposite, or complementary,
calculated to give rise to the particular sort of
relation out of which the enjoyment of a certain mode of self-consciousness will necessarily
spring.   Let this sentence be well pondered
over until the full extent of its significance is
grasped, for it is the key to the whole matter.
Very well, then: Spirit wants to Enjoy Life,
and so, by thinking of itself as *having* the
enjoyment which it wishes, it produces the
conditions which, by their reaction upon itself,
give rise to the reality of the sort of enjoyment
contemplated.   In more scientific language an
opposite polarity is induced, giving rise to a

current which stimulates a particular mode of sensation, which sensation in turn becomes a fresh starting-point for still further action; and in this way each successive stage becomes the stepping-stone to a still higher degree of sensation — that is, to a Fuller Enjoyment of Life.

Such a conception as this presents us with a Progressive Series to which it is impossible to assign any limit. That the progression must be limitless is clear from the fact that there is never any change in the method. At each successive stage the Creating Power is the Self-consciousness of the Spirit, as realized at that stage, still reaching forward for yet further Enjoyment of Life, and so always keeping on repeating the *one* Creative Process at an ever-rising level; and since these are the sole working conditions, the progress is one which logically admits of no finality. And this is where the importance of realizing the Singleness of the Originating Power comes in, for with a Duality each member would limit the other; in fact, Duality as the Originating Power is inconceivable, for, once more to quote "Paddy's Philosophy," "finality would be reached before anything was begun."

This Creative Process, therefore, can only be conceived of as limitless, while at the same time strictly progressive, that is, proceeding stage by stage, each stage being necessary as a preparation for the one that is to follow. Let us then briefly sketch the stages by which things in our world have got as far as they have. The interest of the enquiry lies in the fact that if we can once get at the principle which is producing these results, we may discover some way of giving it personal application.

On the hypothesis of the Self-contemplation of Spirit being the originating power, we have found that a primary ether, or universal substance, is the necessary correspondence to Spirit's simple awareness of its own being. But though awareness of being is the necessary foundation for any further possibilities it is, so to say, not much to talk about. The foundation fact, of course, is to know that I Am; but immediately on this consciousness there follows the desire for Activity — I want to enjoy my I Am-ness by doing something with it. Translating these words into a state of consciousness in the Cosmic Mind they become a Law of Tendency leading to *localized* activity, and, looking only at our own world, this would mean the condensation of the universal etheric substance into the primary nebula which later on becomes our solar system, this being the correspondence to the Self-contemplation of Spirit as passing into specific activity instead of remaining absorbed in simple awareness of Being. Then this self-recognition would lead to the conception of still more specific activity having its appropriate polar opposite, or material correspondence, in the condensation of the nebula into a solar system.

Now at this stage Spirit's conception of itself is that of Activity, and consequently the material correspondence is Motion, as distinguished from the simple diffused ether which is the correspondence of mere awareness of Being. But what sort of motion? Is the material movement evolved at this stage bound to take any particular form? A little consideration will show us that it is. At this initial stage, the first awakening, so to say, of Spirit into activity, its consciousness can only be that of activity *absolute;* that is, not as related to any other mode of activity because as yet there is none, but only as related to an all-embracing

Being; so that the only possible conception of Activity at this stage is that of *Self-sustained* activity, not depending on any preceding mode of activity because there is none. The law of reciprocity therefore demands a similar self-sustained motion in the material correspondence, and mathematical considerations show that the only sort of motion which can sustain a self-supporting body moving *in vacuo* is a rotary motion bringing the body itself into a spherical form. Now this is exactly what we find at both extremes of the material world. At the big end the spheres of the planets rotating on their axes and revolving round the sun; and at the little end the spheres of the atoms consisting of particles which, modern science tells us, in like manner rotate round a common center at distances which are astronomical as compared with their own mass. Thus the two ultimate units of physical manifestation, the atom and the planet, both follow the same law of self-sustained motion which we have found that, on *a priori* grounds, they ought in order to express the primary activity of Spirit. And we may note in passing that this rotary, or *absolute,* motion is the combination of the only two possible *relative* modes of motion, namely, motion from a point and motion to it, that is to say centrifugal and centripetal motion; so that in rotary, or absolute, motion we find that both the polarities of motion are included, thus repeating on the purely mechanical side the primordial principle of the Unity including the Duality in itself.

But the Spirit wants something more than mechanical motion, something more alive than the preliminary Rota, and so the first step toward individualized consciousness meets us in plant life. Then on the principle that each successive stage affords the platform for a further outlook, plant life is followed by animal life, and this by the Human order in which the liberty of selecting its own conditions is immensely extended. In this way the Spirit's expression of itself has now reached the point where its polar complementary, or Reciprocal, manifests as Intellectual Man — thus constituting the Fourth great stage of Spirit's Self-recognition. But the Creative Process cannot stop here, for, as we have seen, its root in the Self-contemplation of Spirit renders it of necessity an Infinite Progression. So it is no use asking what is its ultimate, for it has no ultimate — its word is " Excelsior "— ever

Life and " Life more Abundant." Therefore
the question is not as to finality where there is
none, but as to the next step in the progression.
Four kingdoms we know: what is to be the
Fifth? All along the line the progress has
been in one direction, namely, toward the
development of more perfect Individuality,
and therefore on the principle of continuity we
may reasonably infer that the next stage will
take us still further in the same direction. We
want something more perfect than we have yet
reached, but our ideas as to what it should be
are very various, not to say discordant, for
one person's idea of better is another person's
idea of worse. Therefore what we want to
get at is some broad generalization of principle
which will be in advance of our past experiences. This means that we must look for this
principle in something that we have not yet
experienced, and the only place where we can
possibly find principles which have not yet
manifested themselves is *in gremio Dei* — that
is, in the innermost of the Originating Spirit,
or as St. John calls it, " in the bosom of the
Father." So we are logically brought to personal participation in the Divine Ideal as the
only principle by which the advance into the

next stage can possibly be made.   Therefore we arrive at the question, What is the Divine Ideal like?

CHAPTER III

THE DIVINE IDEAL

WHAT is the Divine Ideal? At first it might appear hopeless to attempt to answer such a question, but by adhering to a definite principle we shall find that it will open out, and lead us on, and show us things which we could not otherwise have seen — this is the nature of principle, and is what distinguishes it from mere rules which are only the application of principle under some particular set of conditions. We found two principles as essential in our conception of the Originating Spirit, namely its power of Selection and its power of Initiative; and we found a third principle as its only possible Motive, namely the Desire of the LIVING for ever increasing Enjoyment of Life. Now with these three principles as the very essence of the All-originating Spirit to guide us, we shall, I think, be able to form some conception of that Divine Ideal which gives rise to the Fifth Stage of Manifestation of Spirit, upon which we should now be preparing to enter.

We have seen that the Spirit's Enjoyment of Life is necessarily a *reciprocal* — it must have a corresponding fact in manifestation to answer to it; otherwise by the inherent law of mind no consciousness, and consequently no enjoyment, could accrue; and therefore by the law of continuous progression the required Reciprocal should manifest as a being awakening to the consciousness of the principle by which he himself comes into existence.

Such an awakening cannot proceed from a comparison of one set of existing conditions with another, but only from the recognition of a Power which is independent of all conditions, that is to say, the absolute Self-dependence of the Spirit. A being thus awakened would be the proper correspondence of the Spirit's Enjoyment of Life at a stage not only above mechanical motion or physical vitality, but even above intellectual perception of existing phenomena, that is to say at the stage where the Spirit's Enjoyment consists in recognizing itself as the Source of all things. The position in the Absolute would be, so to speak, the awakening of Spirit to the recognition of its own Artistic Ability. I use the word " Artistic " as more nearly expressing an almost unstatable idea than any other I can think of, for the work of the artist approaches more closely to creation *ex nihilo* than any other form of human activity. The work of the artist is the expression of the self that the artist is, while that of the scientist is the comparison of facts which exist independently of his own personality. It is true that the realm of Art is not without its methods of analysis, but the analysis is that of the artist's own feeling and of the causes which give rise to it. These are found to contain in themselves certain principles which are fundamental to all Art, but these principles are the laws of the creative action of mind rather than those of the limitations of matter. Now if we may transfer this familiar analogy to our conception of the working of the All-Originating Mind we may picture it as the Great Artist giving visible expression to His feeling by a process which, though subject to no restriction from antecedent conditions, yet works by a Law which is inseparable from the Feeling itself — in fact the Law *is* the Feeling, and the

Feeling *is* the Law, the Law of Perfect Creativeness.

Some such Self-contemplation as this is the only way in which we can conceive the next, or Fifth, stage of Spirit's Self-recognition as taking place. Having got as far as it has in the four previous stages, that is to the production of intellectual man as its correspondence, the next step in advance must be on the lines I have indicated — unless, indeed, there were a sudden and arbitrary breaking of the Law of Continuity, a supposition which the whole Creative Process up to now forbids us to entertain. Therefore we may picture the Fifth stage of the Self-contemplation of Spirit as its awakening to the recognition of its own Artistic Ability, its own absolute freedom of action and creative power — just as in studio parlance we say that an artist becomes " free of his palette." But by the always present Law of Reciprocity, through which alone self-consciousness can be attained, this Self-recognition of Spirit in the Absolute implies a corresponding objective fact in the world of the Relative; that is to say, the coming into manifestation of a being capable of realizing the Free Creative Artistry of the Spirit, and of recognizing the same principle in himself, while at the same time realizing also the *relation* between the Universal Manifesting Principle and its Individual Manifestation.

Such, it appears to me, must be the conception of the Divine Ideal embodied in the Fifth Stage of the progress of manifestation. But I would draw particular attention to the concluding words of the last paragraph, for if we miss the *relation* between the Universal Manifesting Principle and its Individual Manifestation, we have failed to realize the Principle altogether, whether in the Universal or in the Individual — it is just their interaction that makes each become what it does become — and in this further becoming consists the progression. This relation proceeds from the principle I pointed out in the opening chapter which makes it necessary for the Universal Spirit to be always harmonious with itself; and if this Unity is not recognized by the individual he cannot hold that position of Reciprocity to the Originating Spirit which will enable it to recognize itself as in the Enjoyment of Life at the higher level we are now contemplating — rather the feeling conveyed would be that of something antagonistic, producing the reverse of enjoyment, thus philosophically bringing out the point of the Scriptural injunction, "Grieve not the Spirit." Also the reaction upon the individual must necessarily give rise to a corresponding state of inharmony, though he may not be able to define his feeling of unrest or to account for it. But on the other hand if the grand harmony of the Originating Spirit within itself is duly regarded, then the individual mind affords a fresh center from which the Spirit contemplates itself in what I have ventured to call its Artistic Originality — a boundless potential of Creativeness, yet always regulated by its own inherent Law of Unity.

And this Law of the Spirit's Original Unity is a very simple one. It is the Spirit's necessary and basic conception of itself. A lie is a statement that something is, which is not. Then, since the Spirit's statement or conception of anything necessarily makes that thing exist, it is logically impossible for it to conceive a lie. Therefore the Spirit is Truth. Similarly disease and death are the negative of Life, and therefore the Spirit, as the Principle of Life, cannot embody disease or death in its Self-contemplation. In like manner also, since it is free to produce what it will, the Spirit cannot desire the presence of repugnant forms, and so one of its inherent Laws must be Beauty. In this threefold Law of Truth, Life, and Beauty, we find the whole underlying nature of the Spirit, and no action on the part of the individual can be at variance with the Originating Unity which does not contravert these fundamental principles.

This it will be seen leaves the individual absolutely unfettered except in the direction of breaking up the fundamental harmony on which he himself, as included in the general creation, is dependent. This certainly cannot be called limitation, and we are all free to follow the lines of our own individuality in every other direction; so that, although the recognition of our relation to the Originating Spirit safeguards us from injuring ourselves or others, it in no way restricts our liberty of action or narrows our field of development. Am I, then, trying to base my action upon a fundamental desire for the opening out of Truth, for the increasing of Livingness, and for the creating of Beauty? Have I got this as an ever present Law of Tendency at the back of my thought? If so, then this law

will occupy precisely the same place in My
Microcosm, or personal world, that it does in
the Macrocosm, or great world, as a power
which is in itself formless, but which by reason of its presence necessarily impresses its
character upon all that the creative energy
forms. On this basis the creative energy of
the Universal Mind may be safely trusted to
work through the specializing influence of our
own thought [1] and we may adopt the maxim
" trust your desires " because we know that
they are the movement of the Universal in
ourselves, and that being based upon our
fundamental recognition of the Life, Love,
and Beauty which the Spirit is, their unfoldments must carry these initial qualities with
them all down the line, and thus, in however
small a degree, becomes a portion of the working of the Spirit in its inherent creativeness.

This perpetual Creativeness of the Spirit is
what we must never lose sight of, and that is
why I want the student to grasp clearly the
idea of the Spirit's Self-contemplation as the
only possible root of the Creative Process.
Not only at the first creation of the world, but
at all times the plane of the innermost is that

[1] See my Doré Lectures, 1909.

of Pure Spirit,[1] and therefore at this, the originating point, there is nothing else for Spirit to contemplate excepting itself; then this Self-contemplation produces corresponding manifestation, and since Self-contemplation or recognition of its own existence must necessarily go on continually, the corresponding creativeness must always be at work. If this fundamental idea be clearly grasped we shall see that incessant and progressive creativeness is the very essence and being of Spirit. This is what is meant by the Affirmativeness of the Spirit. It cannot *per se* act negatively, that is to say uncreatively, for by the very nature of its Self-recognition such a negative action would be impossible. Of course if *we* act negatively then, since the Spirit is always acting affirmatively, we are moving in the opposite direction to it; and consequently so long as we regard our own negative action as being affirmative, the Spirit's action must appear to us negative, and thus it is that all the negative conditions of the world have their root in negative or inverted thought but the more we bring our thought into harmony with the Life, Love, and Beauty which the Spirit is, the less

[1] See my Edinburgh Lectures on Mental Science.

these inverted conditions will obtain, until at last they will be eliminated altogether. To accomplish this is our great object; for though the progress may be slow it will be steady if we proceed on a definite principle; and to lay hold of the true principle is the purpose of our studies. And the principle to lay hold of is the Ceaseless Creativeness of Spirit. This is what we mean when we speak of it as The Spirit of the Affirmative, and I would ask my readers to impress this term upon their minds. Once grant that the All-originating Spirit is thus the Spirit of the Pure Affirmative, and we shall find that this will lead us logically to results of the highest value.

If, then, we keep this Perpetual and Progressive Creativeness of the Spirit continually in mind we may rely upon its working as surely in ourselves as in that great cosmic forward movement which we speak of as Evolution. It is the same power of Evolution working within ourselves, only with this difference, that in proportion as we come to realize its nature we find ourselves able to facilitate its progress by offering more and more favorable conditions for its working. We do not add to the force of the Power, for we are products of it and so cannot generate what generates *us;* but by providing suitable conditions we can more and more highly specialize it. This is the method of all the advance that has ever been made. We never create any force (*e.g.* electricity) but we provide special conditions under which the force manifests *itself* in a variety of useful and beautiful ways, unsuspected possibilities which lay hidden in the power until brought to light by the cooperation of the Personal Factor.

Now it is precisely the introduction [1] of this Personal Factor that concerns us, because to all eternity we can only recognize things from our own center of consciousness, whether in this world or in any other; therefore the practical question is how to specialize in our own case the *generic* Originating Life which, when we give it a name, we call " the Spirit." The method of doing this is perfectly logical when we once see that the principle involved is that of the Self-recognition of Spirit. We have traced the *modus operandi* of the Creative Process sufficiently far to see that the existence of the cosmos is the result of the Spirit's seeing itself *in* the cosmos, and if this be the law

[1] See my Doré Lectures, 1909.

of the whole it must also be the law of the part. But there is this difference, that so long as the normal average relation of particles is maintained the whole continues to subsist, no matter what position any particular particle may go into, just as a fountain continues to exist no matter whether any particular drop of water is down in the basin or at the top of the jet. This is the *generic* action which keeps the race going as a whole. But the question is, What is going to become of ourselves? Then because the law of the whole is also the law of the part we may at once say that what is wanted is for the Spirit *to see itself in us* — in other words, to find in us the Reciprocal which, as we have seen, is necessary to its Enjoyment of a certain Quality of Consciousness. Now, the fundamental consciousness of the Spirit must be that of Self-sustaining Life, and for the full enjoyment of this consciousness there must be a corresponding *individual* consciousness reciprocating it; and on the part of the individual such a consciousness can only arise from the recognition that his own life is identical with that of the Spirit — not something sent forth to wander away by itself, but something included in and forming part of the

Greater Life. Then by the very conditions of the case, such a contemplation on the part of the individual is nothing else than the Spirit contemplating itself from the standpoint of the individual consciousness, and thus fulfilling the Law of the Creative Process under such specialized conditions as must logically result in the perpetuation of the individual life. It is the Law of the Cosmic Creative Process transferred to the individual.

This, it seems to me, is the Divine Ideal: that of an Individuality which recognizes its Source, and recognizes also the method by which it springs from that Source, and which is therefore able to open up in itself a channel by which that Source can flow in uninterruptedly; with the result that from the moment of this recognition the individual lives directly from the Originating Life, as being himself *a special direct creation,* and not merely as being a member of a generic race. The individual who has reached this stage of recognition thus finds a principle of enduring life *within himself;* so then the next question is in what way this principle is likely to manifest itself.

CHAPTER IV

THE MANIFESTATION OF THE LIFE PRINCIPLE

WE must bear in mind that what we have now reached is a principle, or universal potential, only we have located it in the individual. But a principle, as such, is not manifestation. Manifestation is the growth proceeding *from* the principle, that is to say, some Form in which the principle becomes active. At the same time we must recollect that, though *a* form is necessary for manifestation, *the* form is not essential, for the same principle may manifest through various forms, just as electricity may work either through a lamp or a tram-car without in any way changing its inherent nature. In this way we are brought to the conclusion that the Life-principle must always provide itself with a body in which to function, though it does not follow that this body must always be of the same chemical constitution

46

as the one we now possess. We might well imagine some distant planet where the chemical combinations with which we are familiar on earth did not obtain; but if the essential life-principle of any individual were transported thither, then by the Law of the Creative Process it would proceed to clothe itself with a material body drawn from the atmosphere and substance of that planet; and the personality thus produced would be quite at home there, for all his surroundings would be perfectly natural to him, however different the laws of Nature might be there from what we know here.

In such a conception as this we find the importance of the two leading principles to which I have drawn attention — first, the power of the Spirit to create *ex nihilo,* and secondly, the individual's recognition of the basic principle of Unity giving permanence and solidity to the frame of Nature. By the former the self-recognizing life-principle could produce any sort of body it chose; and by the latter it would be led to project one in harmony with the natural order of the particular planet, thus making all the facts of that order solid realities to the individual, and himself a solid and natural being to the other inhabitants of that world. But this would not do away with the individual's knowledge of how he got there; and so, supposing him to have realized his identity with the Universal Life-Principle sufficiently to consciously control the projection of his own body, he could at will disintegrate the body which accorded with the conditions of one planet and constitute one which accorded just as harmoniously with those of another, and could thus function on any number of planets as a perfectly natural being on each of them. He would in all respects resemble the other inhabitants with one all-important exception, that since he had attained to unity with his Creative Principle he would not be tied by the laws of matter as they were.

Any one who should attain to such a power could only do so by his realization of the all-embracing Unity of the Spirit as being the Foundation of all things; and this being the basis of his own extended powers he would be the last to controvert his own basic principle by employing his powers in such a way as to disturb the natural course of evolution in the world where he was. He might use them to help forward the evolution of others in that world, but certainly never to disturb it, for he would always act on the maxim that " Order is Heaven's First Law."

Our object, however, is not to transfer ourselves to other planets but to get the best out of this one; but we shall not get the best out of this one until we realize that the power which will enable us to do so is so absolutely universal and fundamental that its application in this world is precisely the same as in any other, and that is why I have stated it as a general proposition applicable to all worlds.

The principle being thus universal there is no reason why we should postpone its application till we find ourselves in another world, and the best place and time to begin are Here and Now. The starting point is not in time or locality, but in the mode of Thought; and if we realize that this Point of Origination is Spirit's power to produce something out of nothing, and that it does this in accordance with the natural order of substance of the particular world in which it is working, then the spiritual ego in ourselves, as proceeding direct from the Universal Spirit, should be able first, to so harmoniously combine the working of spiritual and physical laws in its own body as to keep it in perfect health, secondly to carry this process further and renew the body, thus eradicating the effects of old age, and thirdly to carry the process still further and perpetuate this renewed body as long as the individual might desire.

If the student shows this to one of his average acquaintances who has never given any thought to these things, his friend will undoubtedly exclaim " Tommy rot! " even if he does not use a stronger expletive. He will at once appeal to the past experience of all mankind, his argument being that what has not been in the past cannot be in the future; yet he does not apply the same argument to aeronautics and is quite oblivious of the fact that the Sacred Volume which he reverences contains promises of these very things. The really earnest student must never forget the maxim that " Principle is not bound by Precedent "—if it were we should still be primitive savages.

To use the Creative Process we must Affirm the Creative Power, that is to say, we must go back to the Beginning of the series and start with Pure Spirit, only remembering that this starting-point is now to be found *in ourselves,* for this is what distinguishes the individual Creative Process from the cosmic one. This is where the importance of realizing only ONE Originating Power instead of two interacting powers comes in, for it means that we do not derive our power from any existing polarity, but that we are going to establish polarities which will start secondary causation on the lines which we thus determine. This also is where the importance comes in of recognizing that the only possible originating movement of spirit must be Self-contemplation, for this shows us that we do not have to contemplate existing conditions but the Divine Ideal, and that this contemplation of the Divine Ideal of Man is the Self-contemplation of the Spirit from the standpoint of Human Individuality.

Then the question arises, if these principles are true, why are we not demonstrating them? Well, when our fundamental principle is obviously correct and yet we do not get the proper results, the only inference is that somewhere or other we have introduced something antagonistic to the fundamental principle, something not inherent in the principle itself and which therefore owes its presence to some action of our own. Now the error consists in the belief that the Creative Power is limited by the material in which it works. If this be assumed, then you have to calculate the resistances offered by the material; and since by the terms of the Creative Process these resistances do not really exist, you have no basis of calculation at all — in fact you have no means of knowing where you are, and everything is in confusion. This is why it is so important to remember that the Creative Process is the action of a Single Power, and that the interaction of two opposite polarities comes in at a later stage, and is not creative, but only distributive — that is to say, it localizes the Energy already proceeding from the Single Power. This is a fundamental truth which should never be lost sight of. So long, however, as we fail to see this truth we necessarily limit the Creative Power by the material it works in, and in practise we do this by referring to past experience as the only standard of judgment. We are measuring the Fifth Kingdom by the standard of the Fourth, as though we should say that an intellectual man, a being of the Fourth Kingdom, was to be limited by the conditions which obtain in the

First or Mineral Kingdom — to use Scriptural language we are seeking the Living among the dead.

And moreover at the present time a new order of experience is beginning to open out to us, for well authenticated instances of the cure of disease by the invisible power of the Spirit are steadily increasing in number. The facts are now too patent to be denied — what we want is a better knowledge of the power which accounts for them. And if this beginning is now with us, by what reason can we limit it? The difference between the healing of disease and the renewal of the entire organism and the perpetuation of life is only a difference of degree and not of kind; so that the actual experience of increasing numbers shows the working of a principle to which we can logically set no limits.

If we get the steps of the Creative Process clearly into our minds we shall see why we have hitherto had such small results.

> Spirit creates by Self-contemplation;
> Therefore, What it contemplates itself
>   as being, that it becomes.
> You are individualized Spirit;
> Therefore, What you contemplate as

the Law of your being becomes the Law of your being.

Hence, contemplate a Law of Death arising out of the Forces of the Material reacting against the Power of the Spirit and overcoming it, and you impress this mode of self-recognition upon Spirit in yourself. Of course you cannot alter its inherent nature, but you cause it to work under negative conditions and thus make it produce negative results so far as you yourself are concerned.

But reverse the process, and contemplate a Law of Life as inherent in the very Being of the Spirit, and therefore as inherent in spirit in yourself; and contemplate the forces of the Material as practically non-existent in the Creative Process, because they are products of it and not causes — look at things in this way and you will impress a corresponding conception upon the Spirit which, by the Law of Reciprocity, thus enters into Self-contemplation on *these* lines from the standpoint of your own individuality; and then by the nature of the Creative Process a corresponding externalization is bound to take place. Thus our initial question, How did anything come into existence at all, brings us to the recognition

of a Law of Life which we may each specialize
for ourselves; and in the degree to which we
specialize it we shall find the Creative Principle
at work within us building up a healthier and
happier personality in mind, body, and circumstances.

Only we must learn to distinguish the vehicles of Spirit from Spirit itself, for the distinction has very important bearings. What
distinguishes the vehicles from the Spirit is the
Law of Growth. The Spirit is the Formless
principle of Life, and the vehicle is a Form in
which this principle functions. Now the vehicle is a projection by the Spirit of substance
coordinate with the natural order of the plane
on which the vehicle functions, and therefore
requires to be built up comformably to that
order. This building up is what we speak
of as Growth; and since the principle which
causes the growth is the individualized Spirit,
the rate at which the growth will go on will
depend on the amount of vitalizing energy the
Spirit puts into it, and the amount of vitalizing
energy will depend on the degree in which the
individualized Spirit appreciates its own livingness, and finally the degree of this appreciation
will depend on the quality of the individual's

perception of the Great All-originating Spirit as reflecting itself in him and thus making his contemplation of It nothing else than the Creative Self-contemplation of the Spirit proceeding from an individual and personal center.

We must therefore not omit the Law of Growth in the vehicle from our conception of the working of the Spirit. As a matter of fact the vehicle has nothing to say in the matter for it is simply a projection from the Spirit; but for this very reason its formation will be slow or rapid in exact proportion to the individual spirit's vitalizing conception. We could imagine a degree of vitalizing conception that would produce the corresponding form instantaneously, but at present we must allow for the weakness of our spiritual power — not as thinking it by any means incapable of accomplishing its object, but as being far slower in operation now than we hope to see it in the future — and so we must not allow ourselves to be discouraged, but must hold our thought knowing that it is doing its creative work, and that the corresponding growth is slowly but surely taking place — thus following the Divine precept that men ought always to pray and not to faint. Gradually as we gain experience on these new lines our confidence in the power of the Spirit will increase, and we shall be less inclined to argue from the negative side of things, and thus the hindrances to the inflow of the Originating Spirit will be more and more removed, and greater and greater results will be obtained.

If we would have our minds clear on this subject of Manifestation we should remember its threefold nature: — First the General Life-Principle, secondly the Localization of this principle in the Individual, and thirdly the Growth of the Vehicle as it is projected by the individualized spirit with more or less energy. It is a sequence of progressive condensation from the Undifferentiated Universal Spirit to the ultimate and outermost vehicle — a truth enshrined in the esoteric maxim that " Matter is Spirit at its lowest level."

The forms thus produced are in true accord with the general order of Nature on the particular plane where they occur, and are therefore perfectly different from forms temporarily consolidated out of material drawn from other living organisms. These latter phantasmal bodies are held together only by an act of concentrated volition, and can therefore only be maintained for a short time and with effort; while the body which the individualized spirit, or ego, builds for itself is produced by a perfectly natural process and does not require any effort to sustain it, since it is kept in touch with the whole system of the planet by the continuous and effortless action of the individual's sub-conscious mind.

This is where the action of sub-conscious mind as the builder of the body comes in. Sub-conscious mind acts in accordance with the aggregate of suggestion impressed upon it by the conscious mind, and if this suggestion is that of perfect harmony with the physical laws of the planet then a corresponding building by the sub-conscious mind will take place, a process which, so far from implying any effort, consists rather in a restful sense of unity with Nature.[1]

And if to this sense of union with the Soul of Nature, that Universal Sub-conscious Mind which holds in the cosmos the same place that the sub-conscious mind does in ourselves — if to this there be superadded a sense of union with the All-creating Spirit from which the

[1] For the relation between conscious and sub-conscious mind see my " Edinburgh Lectures on Mental Science."

Soul of Nature flows, then through the medium of the individual's sub-conscious mind such specialized effects can be produced in his body as to transcend our past experiences without in any way violating the order of the universe. The Old Law was the manifestation of the Principle of Life working under constricted conditions: the New Law is the manifestation of the same Principle working under expanding conditions. Thus it is that though God never changes we are said to " increase with the increase of God."

CHAPTER V

THE PERSONAL FACTOR

I HAVE already pointed out that the presence
of a single all-embracing Cosmic Mind is an
absolute necessity for the existence of any
creation whatever, for the reason that if each
individual mind were an entirely separate
center of perception, not linked to all other
minds by a common ground of underlying
mentality independent of all individual action,
then no two persons would see the same thing
at the same time, in fact no two individuals
would be conscious of living in the same world.
If this were the case there would be no common standard to which to refer our sensations;
and, indeed, coming into existence with no
consciousness of environment except such as
we could form by our own unaided thought,
and having by the hypothesis no standard by
which to form our thoughts, we could not
form the conception of any environment at

all, and consequently could have no recognition
of our own existence. The confusion of
thought involved even in the attempt to state
such a condition shows it to be perfectly inconceivable, for the simple reason that it is
self-contradictory and self-destructive. On
this account it is clear that our own existence
and that of the world around us necessarily
implies the presence of a Universal Mind acting on certain *fixed lines of its own* which
establish the basis for the working of all individual minds. This paramount action of the
Universal Mind thus sets an unchangeable
standard by which all individual mental action
must eventually be measured, and therefore
our first concern is to ascertain what this
standard is and to make it the basis of our own
action.

But if the independent existence of a common standard of reference is necessary for
our self-recognition simply as inhabitants of
the world we live in, then *a fortiori* a common
standard of reference is necessary for our
recognition of the unique place we hold in the
Creative Order, which is that of introducing
the Personal Factor without which the possibilities contained in the great Cosmic Laws

would remain undeveloped, and the Self-contemplation of Spirit could never reach those infinite unfoldments of which it is logically capable.

The evolution of the Personal Factor is therefore the point with which we are most concerned. As a matter of fact, whatever theories we may hold to the contrary, we do all realize the same cosmic environment in the same way; that is to say, our minds all act according to certain generic laws which underlie all our individual diversities of thought and feeling. This is so because we are made that way and cannot help it. But with the Personal Factor the case is different. A standard is no less necessary, but we are not so made as to conform to it automatically. The very conception of automatic conformity to a *personal* standard is self-contradictory, for it does away with the very thing that constitutes personality, namely freedom of volition, the use of the powers of Initiative and Selection. For this reason conformity to the Standard of Personality must be a matter of choice, which amounts to the same thing as saying that it rests with each individual to form his own conception of a standard of Personality; but which liberty, however, carries with it the inevitable result that we shall bring into manifestation the *conditions* corresponding to the sort of personality we accept as our normal standard.

I would draw attention to the words "Normal Standard." What we shall eventually attain is, not what we merely wish, but what we regard as normal. The reason is that since we subconsciously know ourselves to be based upon the inherent Law of the Universal Mind we feel, whether we can reason it out or not, that we cannot force the All-producing Mind to work contrary to its own inherent qualities, and therefore we intuitively recognize that we cannot transcend the sort of personality which is normal according to the Law of Universal Mind. This thought is always at the back of our mind and we cannot get away from it for the simple reason that it is inherent in our mental constitution, because our mind is itself a product of the Creative Process; and to suppose ourselves transcending the possibilities contained in the Originating Mind would involve the absurdity of supposing that we can get the greater out of the less.

Nevertheless there are some who try to do so, and their position is as follows. They say in effect, I want to transcend the standard of humanity as I see it around me. But this is the normal standard according to the Law of the Universe, therefore I have to get above the Law of the Universe. Consequently I cannot draw the necessary power from that Law, and so there is nowhere else to get it except from myself. Thus the aspirant is thrown back upon his own individual will as the ultimate power, with the result that the onus lies on him of concentrating a force sufficient to overcome the Law of the Universe. There is thus continually present to him a suggestion of struggle against a tremendous opposing force, and as a consequence he is continually subjecting himself to a strain which grows more and more intense as he realizes the magnitude of the force against which he is contending. Then as he begins to realize the inequality of the struggle he seeks for extraneous aid, and so he falls back on various expedients, all of which have this in common that they ultimately amount to invoking the assistance of other individualities, not seeing that this involves the same fallacy which has brought him to his present straits, the fallacy, namely, of supposing that any individuality can develop a power greater than that of the source from which itself proceeds. The fallacy is a radical one; and therefore all efforts based upon it are fore-doomed to ultimate failure, whether they take the form of reliance on personal force of will, or magical rites, or austerity practised against the body, or attempts by abnormal concentration to absorb the individual in the universal, or the invocation of spirits, or any other method — the same fallacy is involved in them all, that the less is larger than the greater.

Now the point to be noted is that the idea of transcending the present conditions of humanity does not necessarily imply the idea of transcending the normal law of humanity. The mistake we have hitherto made has been in fixing the Standard of Personality too low and in taking our past experiences as measuring the ultimate possibilities of the race. Our liberty consists in our ability to form our own conception of the Normal Standard of Personality, only subject to the conditions arising out of the inherent Law of the underlying Universal Mind; and so the whole thing resolves itself into the question, What are those fundamental conditions? The Law is that we cannot transcend the Normal; therefore comes the question, What is the Normal?

I have endeavored to answer this question in the chapter on the Divine Ideal, but since this is the crucial point of the whole subject we may devote a little further attention to it. The Normal Standard of Personality must necessarily be the reproduction in Individuality of what the Universal Mind is in itself, because, by the nature of the Creative Process, this standard results from Spirit's Self-contemplation at the stage where its recognition is turned toward its own power of Initiative and Selection. At this stage Spirit's Self-recognition has passed beyond that of Self-expression through a mere Law of Averages into the recognition of what I have ventured to call its Artistic Ability; and as we have seen that Self-recognition at any stage can only be attained by the realization of a *relation* stimulating that particular sort of consciousness, it follows that for the purpose of this further advance expression through individuals of a corresponding type is a necessity. Then by the Law of Reciprocity such beings must possess powers similar to those contemplated in itself by the Originating Spirit, in other words they must be in their own sphere the image and likeness of the Spirit as it sees itself.

Now we have seen that the Creating Spirit necessarily possesses the powers of Initiative and Selection. These we may call its *active* properties — the summing up of what it *does*. But what any power does depends on what it *is*, for the simple reason that it cannot give out what it does not contain; therefore at the back of the initiative and selective power of the Spirit we must find what the Spirit *is*, namely, what are its *substantive* properties. To begin with it must be Life. Then because it is Life it must be Love, because as the undifferentiated Principle of Life it cannot do otherwise than tend to the fuller development of life in each individual, and the pure motive of giving greater enjoyment of life is Love. Then because it is Life guided by Love it must also be Light, that is to say, the primary all-inclusive perception of boundless manifestations yet to be. Then from this proceeds Power, because there is no opposing force at the level of Pure Spirit; and therefore Life urged forward by Love or the desire for recognition, and by Light or the pure perception of the Law of Infinite Possibility, must necessarily produce Power, for the simple reason that under these conditions it could not stop short of action, for that would be the denial of the Life, Love, and Light which it is. Then because the Spirit is Life, Love, Light, and Power, it is also Peace, again for a very simple reason, that being the Spirit of the Whole it cannot set one part in antagonism against another, for that would be to destroy the wholeness. Next the Spirit must be Beauty, because on the same principle of Wholeness it must duly proportion every part to every other part, and the due proportioning of all parts is beauty. And lastly the Spirit must be Joy, because, working on these lines, it cannot do otherwise than find pleasure in the Self-expression which its works afford it, and in the contemplation of the limitlessness of the Creative Process by which each realized stage of evolution, however excellent, is still the stepping-stone to something yet more excellent, and so on in everlasting progression.

For these reasons we may sum up the Substantive Being of the All-originating Spirit as Life, Love, Light, Power, Peace, Beauty, and

Joy; and its Active Power as that of Initiative and Selection. These, therefore, constitute the basic laws of the underlying universal mentality which sets the Standard of Normal Personality — a standard which, when seen in this light, transcends the utmost scope of our thought, for it is nothing else than the Spirit of the Infinite Affirmative conceived in Human Personality. This standard is therefore that of the Universal Spirit itself reproduced in Human Individuality by the same Law of Reciprocity which we have found to be the fundamental law of the Creative Process — only now we are tracing the action of this Law in the Fifth Kingdom instead of in the Fourth.

This Standard, then, we may call the Universal Principle of Humanity, and having now traced the successive steps by which it is reached from the first cosmic movement of the Spirit in the formation of the primary nebula, we need not go over the old ground again, and may henceforward take this Divine Principle of Humanity as our Normal Standard and make it the starting point for our further evolution. But how are we to do this? Simply by using the one method of Creative Process, that is, the Self-contemplation of Spirit.

We now know ourselves to be Reciprocals of the Divine Spirit, centers in which It finds a fresh standpoint for Self-contemplation; and so the way to rise to the heights of this Great Pattern is by contemplating it as the Normal Standard of our own Personality.

And be it noted that the Pattern thus set before us is Universal. It is the embodiment of all the great principles of the Affirmative, and so in no way interferes with our own particular individuality — *that* is something built up upon this foundation, something additional affording the differentiating medium through which this unifying Principle finds variety of expression, therefore we need be under no apprehension lest by resting upon this Pattern we should become less ourselves. On the contrary the recognition of it sets us at liberty to become more fully ourselves because we know that we are basing our development, not upon the strength of our own unaided will, nor yet upon any sort of extraneous help, but upon the Universal Law itself, manifesting through us in the proper sequence of the Creative Order; so that we are still dealing with Universal principles, only the principle by which we are now working is the Universal Principle of Personality.

I wish the student to get this idea very clearly because this is really the crux of the passage from the Fourth Kingdom into the Fifth. The great problem of the future of evolution is the introduction of the Personal Factor. The reason why this is so is very simple when we see it. To take a thought from my own "Doré Lectures" we may put it in this way. In former days no one thought of building ships of iron because iron does not float; yet now ships are seldom built of anything else, though the relative specific gravities of iron and water remain unchanged. What has changed is the Personal Factor. It has expanded to a more intelligent perception of the law of flotation, and we now see that wood floats and iron sinks, both of them by the same principle working under opposite conditions, the law, namely, that anything will float which bulk for bulk is lighter than the volume of water displaced by it, so that by including in our calculations the displacement of the vessel as well as the specific gravity of the material, we now make iron float by the very same law by which it sinks. This example shows that the function of the Personal Factor is to analyze the manifestations of Law which are spontaneously afforded by Nature and to discover the Universal Affirmative Principle which lies hidden within them, and then by the exercise of our powers of Initiative and Selection to provide such specialized conditions as will enable the Universal Principle to work in perfectly new ways transcending anything in our past experience. This is how all progress has been achieved up to the present; and is the way in which all progress must be achieved in the future, only for the purpose of evolution, or growth from within, we must transfer the method to the spiritual plane.

The function, then, of the Personal Factor in the Creative Order is to provide specialized conditions by the use of the powers of Selection and Initiative, a truth indicated by the maxim " Nature unaided fails "; but the difficulty is that if enhanced powers were attained by the whole population of the world without any common basis for their use, their promiscuous exercise could only result in chaotic confusion and the destruction of the entire race. To introduce the creative power of the

Individual and at the same time avoid converting it into a devastating flood is the great problem of the transition from the Fourth Kingdom into the Fifth. For this purpose it becomes necessary to have a Standard of the Personal Factor independent of any individual conceptions, just as we found that in order for us to attain self-consciousness at all it was a necessity that there should be a Universal Mind as the *generic* basis of all individual mentality; only in regard to the generic build of mind the conformity is necessarily automatic, while in regard to the specializing process the fact that the essence of that process is Selection and Initiative renders it impossible for the conformity to the Standard of Personality to be automatic — the very nature of the thing makes it a matter of individual choice.

Now a Standard of Personality independent of individual conceptions must be the *essence* of Personality as distinguished from individual idiosyncrasies, and can therefore be nothing else than the Creative Life, Love, Beauty, etc., viewed as a Divine Individuality, by identifying ourselves with which we eliminate all possibility of conflict with other personalities based on the same fundamental recognition; and the very universality of this Standard allows free play to all our particular idiosyncrasies while at the same time preventing them from antagonizing the fundamental principles to which we have found that the Self-contemplation of the Originating Spirit must necessarily give rise. In this way we attain a Standard of Measurement for our own powers. If we recognize no such Standard our development of spiritual powers, our discovery of the immense possibilities hidden in the inner laws of Nature and of our own being, can only become a scourge to ourselves and others, and it is for this reason that these secrets are so jealously guarded by those who know them, and that over the entrance to the temple are written the words " Eskato Bebeloi "—" Hence ye Profane."

But if we recognize and accept this Standard of Measurement then we need never fear our discovery of hidden powers either in ourselves or in Nature, for on this basis it becomes impossible for us to misuse them. Therefore it is that all systematic teaching on these subjects begins with instruction regarding the Creative Order of the Cosmos, and then proceeds to exhibit the same Order as reproduced on the plane of Personality and so affording a fresh starting point for the Creative Process by the introduction of Individual Initiative and Selection. This is the doctrine of the Macrocosm and the Microcosm; and the transition from the generic working of the Creative Spirit in the Cosmos to its specific working in the Individual is what is meant by the doctrine of the Octave.

CHAPTER VI

The Standard of Personality

We have now got some general idea as to the place of the personal factor in the Creative Order, and so the next question is, How does this affect ourselves? The answer is that if we have grasped the fundamental fact that the moving power in the Creative Process is the self-contemplation of Spirit, and if we also see that, because we are miniature reproductions of the Original Spirit, our contemplation of It becomes Its contemplation of Itself from the standpoint of our own individuality — if we have grasped these fundamental conceptions, then it follows that our process for developing power is to contemplate the Originating Spirit as the source of the power we want to develop. And here we must guard against a mistake which people often make when looking to the Spirit as the source of power. We are apt to regard it as sometimes giving and sometimes withholding power, and consequently are never sure which way it will act. But by so doing we make Spirit contemplate itself as having no definite action at all, as a plus and minus which mutually cancel each other, and therefore by the Law of the Creative Process no result is to be expected. The mistake consists in regarding the power as something separate from the Spirit; whereas by the analysis of the Creative Process which we have now made we see that the Spirit itself *is* the power, because the power comes into existence only through Spirit's self-contemplation. Then the logical inference from this is that by contemplating the Spirit *as* the power, and *vice versa* by contemplating the power *as* the Spirit, a similar power is being generated in ourselves.

Again an important conclusion follows from this, which is that to generate any *particular sort* of power we should contemplate it in the abstract rather than as applied to the particular set of circumstances we have in hand. The circumstances indicate the sort of power we want but they do not help us to generate it; rather they impress us with a sense of something contrary to the power, something which has to be overcome by it, and therefore we should endeavor to dwell on the power *in itself,* and so come into touch with it in its limitless infinitude.

It is here that we begin to find the benefit of a Divine Standard of Human Individuality. That also is an Infinite Principle, and by identifying ourselves with it we bring to bear upon the abstract conception of infinite Impersonal Power a corresponding conception of Infinite Personality, so that we thus import the Personal Factor which is able *to use* the Power without imposing any strain upon ourselves. We know that by the very nature of the Creative Process we are one with the Originating Spirit and therefore one with all the principles of its Being, and consequently one with its Infinite Personality, and therefore our contemplation of it as the Power which we want gives us the power to use that Power.

This is the Self-contemplation of Spirit employed from the individual standpoint for the generating of power. Then comes the application of the power thus generated. But there is only one Creative Process, that of the Self-contemplation of Spirit, and therefore the way to use this process for the application of the power is to contemplate ourselves as surrounded by the conditions which we want to produce. This does not mean that we are to lay down a hard and fast pattern of the conditions and strenuously endeavor to compel the Power to conform its working to every detail of our mental picture — to do so would be to hinder its working and to exhaust ourselves. What we are to dwell upon is the idea of an Infinite Power producing the happiness we desire, and because this Power is also the Forming Power of the universe trusting it to give that form to the conditions which will most perfectly react upon us to produce the particular state of consciousness desired.

Thus neither on the side of in-drawing nor of out-giving is there any constraining of the Power, while in both cases there is an initiative and selective action on the part of the individual — for the generating of power he takes the initiative of invoking it by contemplation, and he makes selection of the sort of power to invoke; while on the giving-out side he makes selection of the purpose for which the Power is to be employed, and takes the initiative by his thought of directing the Power to that purpose. He thus fulfils the fundamental requirements of the Creative Process by exer-

cising Spirit's inherent faculties of initiative
and selection by means of its inherent method,
namely by Self-contemplation. The whole
action is identical in kind with that which
produces the cosmos, and it is now repeated in
miniature for the particular world of the individual; only we must remember that this
miniature reproduction of the Creative Process
is based upon the great fundamental principles
inherent in the Universal Mind, and cannot
be dissociated from them without involving a
conception of the individual which will ultimately be found self-destructive because it cuts
away the foundation on which his individuality
rests.

It will therefore be seen that any individuality based upon the fundamental Standard of
Personality thus involved in the Universal
Mind has reached the basic principle of union
with the Originating Spirit itself, and we are
therefore correct in saying that union is attained through, or by means of, this Standard
Personality. This is a great truth which in
all ages has been set forth under a variety of
symbolic statements; often misunderstood, and
still continuing to be so, though owing to the
inherent vitality of the idea itself even a partial

apprehension of it produces a corresponding measure of good results. This falling short has been occasioned by the failure to recognize an Eternal Principle at the back of the particular statements — in a word the failure to see what they were talking about. All *principles* are eternal in themselves, and this is what distinguishes them from their particular manifestations as laws determined by temporary and local conditions.

If then, we would reach the root of the matter we must penetrate through all verbal statements to an Eternal Principle which is as active now as ever in the past, and which is as available to ourselves as to any who have gone before us. Therefore it is that when we discern an Eternal and Universal Principle of Human Personality as necessarily involved in the Essential Being of the Originating Universal Spirit — *Filius in gremio Patris* — we have discovered the true Normal Standard of Personality. Then because this standard is nothing else than the principle of Personality expanded to infinitude, there is no limit to the expansion which we ourselves may attain by the operation in us of this principle; and so we are never placed in a position of antagonism to the true law of our being, but on the contrary the larger and more fundamental our conception of personal development the greater will be the fulfilment which we give to the Law The Normal Standard of Personality is found to be itself the Law of the Creative Process working at the personal level; and it cannot be subject to limitation for the simple reason that the process being that of the Self-contemplation of Spirit, no limits can possibly be assigned to this contemplation.

We need, therefore, never be afraid of forming too high an idea of human possibilities provided always that we take this standard as the foundation on which to build up the edifice of our personality. And we see that this standard is no arbitrary one but simply the Expression in Personality of the ONE all-embracing Spirit of the Affirmative; and therefore the only limitation implied by conformity to it is that of being prevented from running on lines the opposite of those of the Creative Process, that is to say, from calling into action causes of disintegration and destruction. In the truly Constructive Order, therefore, the Divine Standard of Personality is as really the basis of the development of specific personality as the Universal Mind is the necessary basis of generic mentality; and just as without this generic ultimate of Mind we should none of us see the same world at the same time, and in fact have no consciousness of existence, so apart from this Divine Standard of Personality it is equally impossible for us to specialize the generic law of our being so as to develop all the glorious possibilities that are latent in it.

Only we must never forget the difference between these two statements of the Universal Law — the one is cosmic and generic, common to the whole race, whether they know it or not, a Standard to which we all conform automatically by the mere fact of being human beings; while the other is a personal and individual Standard, automatic conformity to which is impossible because that would imply the loss of those powers of Initiative and Selection which are the very essence of Personality; so that this Standard necessarily implies a personal selection of it in preference to other conceptions of an antagonistic nature.

CHAPTER VII

Race Thought and New Thought

THE steady following up of the successive stages of the Creative Process has led us to the recognition of an Individuality in the All-creating Spirit itself, but an Individuality which is by its very nature Universal, and so cannot be departed from without violating the essential principles on which the further expansion of our own individuality depends. At the same time it is strictly *individual*, for it is the Spirit of Individuality, and is thus to be distinguished from that merely *generic* race-personality which makes us human beings at all. Race-personality is of course the necessary *basis* for the development of this Individuality; but if we do not see that it is only the preliminary to further evolution, any other conception of our personality as members of the race will prevent our advance toward our proper position in the Creative

84

Order, which is that of introducing the Personal Factor by the exercise of our individual power of initiative and selection.

It is on this account that Race-thought, simply as such, is opposed to the attempt of the individual to pass into a higher order of life. It limits him by strong currents of negative suggestion based on the fallacy that the perpetuation of the race requires the death of the individual;[1] and it is only when the individual sees that this is not true, and that his race-nature constitutes the ground out of which his new Individuality is to be formed, that he becomes able to oppose the negative power of race-thought. He does this by destroying it with its own weapon, that is, by finding in the race-nature itself the very material to be used by the Spirit for building-up the New Man. This is a discovery on the spiritual plane equivalent to the discovery on the physical plane that we can make iron float by the same law by which it sinks. It is the discovery that what we call the mortal part of us is capable of being brought under a higher application of the Universal Law of Life, which will transmute it into an immortal principle.

[1] See "Self-Synthesis" by Dr. Cornwall Round.

When we see what we call the mortal part of us in this light we can employ the very principle on which the negative race-thought is founded as a weapon for the destruction of that thought in our own minds.

The basis of the negative race-thought is the idea that physical death is an essential part of the Normal Standard of Personality, and that the body is composed of so much neutral material with which death can do what it likes. But it is precisely this neutrality of matter that makes it just as amenable to the Law of Life as to the Law of Death — it is simply neutral and not an originating power on either side; so then when we realize that our Normal Standard of Personality is not subject to death, but is the Eternal Essence and Being of Life itself, then we see that this neutrality of matter — its inability to make selection or take initiative on its own account — is just what makes it the plastic medium for the expression of Spirit in ourselves.

In this way the generic or race mind in the individual becomes the instrument through which the specializing power of the Spirit works toward the building up of a personality based upon the truly Normal Standard of Individuality which we have found to be inherent in the All-originating Spirit itself: and since the whole question is that of the introduction of the factor of personal individuality into the creative order of causation, this cannot be done by depriving the individual of what makes him a person instead of a thing, namely, the power of conscious initiative and selection.

For this reason the transition from the Fourth Kingdom into the Fifth cannot be forced upon the race either by a Divine fiat or by the generic action of cosmic law, for it is a *specializing* of the cosmic law which can only be effected by *personal* initiative and selection, just as iron can only be made to float under certain specialized conditions; and consequently the passage from the Fourth into the Fifth Kingdom is a strictly individual process which can only be brought about by a personal perception of what the normal standard of the New Individuality really is. This can only be done by the active laying aside of the old race-standard and the conscious adoption of the new one. The student will do well to consider this carefully, for it explains why the race cannot receive the further evolution simply as a race; and also it shows that our further evolution is not into a state of less activity but of greater, not into being less alive but more alive, not into being less ourselves but more ourselves; thus being just the opposite of those systems which present the goal of existence as re-absorption into the undifferentiated Divine essence. On the contrary our further evolution is into greater degrees of conscious activity than we have ever yet known, because it implies our development of greater powers as the consequence of our clearer perception of our true relation to the All-originating Spirit. It is the recognition that we may, and should, measure ourselves by this New Standard instead of by the old race-standard that constitutes the real New Thought. The New Thought which gives New Life to the individual will never be realized so long as we think that it is merely the name of a particular sect, or that it is to be found in the mechanical observance of a set of rules laid down for us by some particular teacher. It is a New Fact in the experience of the individual, the *reason* for which is indeed made clear to him through intellectual perception of the real nature of the Creative Process, but which can become an actual experience only by habitual personal intercourse with that Divine Spirit which is the Life, Love and Beauty that are at the back of the Creative Process and find expression through it.

From this intercourse new thoughts will continually flow in, all of them bearing that vivifying element which is inherent in their source, and the individual will then proceed to work out these new ideas with the knowledge that they have their origin in the selection and initiative power of the All-creating Spirit itself, and in this way by combined meditation and action he will find himself advancing into increasing light, liberty and usefulness. The advance may be almost imperceptible from one day to another, but it will be perceptible at longer intervals, and the one who is thus moving forward with the Spirit of God will on looking back at any time always find that he is getting more livingness out of life than he was a year previously. And this without strenuous effort, for he is not having to manufacture the power from his own resources but only to *receive* it — and as for *using* it, that is only the exercise of the power itself. So following on these lines you will find that Rest and Power are identical; and so you get the real New Thought which grows in Newness every day.

CHAPTER VIII

THE DÉNOUEMENT OF THE CREATIVE PROCESS

THEN comes the question, What should logically be the dénouement of the progression we have been considering? Let us briefly recapitulate the steps of the series. Universal Spirit by Self-contemplation evolves Universal Substance. From this it produces cosmic creation as the expression of itself as functioning in Space and Time. Then from this initial movement it proceeds to more highly specialized modes of Self-contemplation in a continually ascending scale, for the simple reason that self-contemplation admits of no limits and therefore each stage of self-recognition cannot be other than the starting-point for a still more advanced mode of self-contemplation, and so on *ad infinitum*. Thus there is a continuous progress toward more and more highly specialized forms of life, implying greater liberty and wider scope for enjoyment as the capacity of the individual life corresponds to a higher degree of the contemplation of Spirit; and in this way evolution proceeds till it reaches a level where it becomes impossible to go any further except by the exercise of conscious selection and initiative on the part of the individual, while at the same time conforming to the universal principles of which evolution is the expression.

Now ask yourself in what way individual selection and initiative would be likely to act as expressing the Originating Spirit itself? Given the knowledge on the part of the individual that he is able by his power of initiative and selection to draw directly upon the All-originating Spirit of Life, what motive could he have for not doing so? Therefore, granted such a perfect recognition, we should find the individual holding precisely the same place in regard to his own individual world that the All-originating Spirit does to the cosmos; subject only to the same Law of Love, Beauty, &c., which we found to be necessarily inherent in the Creative Spirit — a similarity which would entirely prevent the individual from exercising his otherwise limitless powers in any sort of antagonism to the Spirit of the Great Whole.

At the same time the individual would be quite aware that he was not the Universal Spirit *in propria persona,* but that he was affording expression to it through his individuality. Now Expression is impossible except through Form, and therefore form of some sort is a necessity of individuality. It is just here, then, that we find the importance of that principle of Harmony with Environment of which I spoke earlier, the principle in accordance with which a person who had obtained complete control of matter, if he wished to transport himself to some other planet, would appear there in perfect conformity with all the laws of matter that obtained in that world; though, of course, not subject to any limitation of the Life Principle in himself. He would exhibit the laws of matter as rendered perfect by the Law of Originating Life. But if any one now living on this earth were thus perfectly to realize the Law of Life he would be in precisely the same position *here* as our imaginary visitor to another planet — in other words the dénouement of the Law of Life is not the putting off of the body, but its inclusion as part of the conscious life of the Spirit.

This does not imply any difference in the molecular structure of the body from that of other men, for by the principle of Harmony of which I have just spoken, it would be formed in strict accordance with the laws of matter on the particular planet; though it would not be subject to the limitations resulting from the average man's non-recognition of the power of the Spirit. The man who had thus fully entered into the Fifth Kingdom would recognize that, in its relation to the denser modes of matter his body was of a similar dense mode. That would be its relation to external environment as seen by others. But since the man now knew *himself* as not belonging to these denser modes of manifestation, but as an individualization of Primary Spirit, he would see that relatively to himself all matter was Primary Substance, and that from this point of view any condensations of that substance into atoms, molecules, tissues, and the like counted for nothing — for him the body would be simply Primary Substance entirely responsive to his will. Yet his reverence for the Law of

Harmony would prevent any disposition to play psychic pranks with it, and he would use his power over the body only to meet actual requirements.

In this way, then, we are led to the conclusion that eternal life in an immortal physical body is the logical dénouement of our evolution; and if we reflect that, by the conditions of the case, the owners of such bodies could at will either transport themselves to other worlds or put off the physical body altogether and remain in the purely subjective life while still retaining the power to reclothe themselves in flesh whenever they chose, we shall see that this dénouement of evolution answers all possible questions as to the increase of the race, the final destruction of the planet, and the like.

This, then, is the ultimate which we should keep in view; but the fact remains that, though there may be hidden ones who have thus attained, the bulk of mankind have not, and that the common lot of humanity is to go through the change which we call death. In broad philosophical terms death may be described as the withdrawal of the life into the subjective consciousness to the total exclusion of the objective consciousness. Then by the general law of the relation between subjective and objective mind, the subjective mind severed from its corresponding objective mentality has no means of acquiring fresh impressions *on its own account,* and therefore can only ring the changes on those impressions which it has brought with it from its past life. But these may be of very various sorts, ranging from the lowest to the highest, from those most opposed to that ultimate destiny of man which we have just been considering, to those which recognize his possibilities in a very large measure, needing little more to bring about the full fruition of perfected life. But however various may be their experiences, all who have passed through death must have this in common that they have lost their physical instrument of objective perception and so have their mode of consciousness determined entirely by the dominant mode of suggestion which they have brought over with them from the objective side of life.[1] Of course if the objective mentality were also brought over this would give the individual the same power of initiative and selection that he possesses while in the body, and, as we

[1] For the relation between subjective and objective mind see my " Edinburgh Lectures on Mental Science."

shall see later on, there are exceptional persons with whom this is the case; but for the great majority the physical brain is a mecessity for the working of the objective mentality, and so when they are deprived of this instrument their life becomes purely subjective and is a sort of dream-life, only with a vast difference between two classes of dreamers — those who dream as they must and those who dream as they will. The former are those who have enslaved themselves in various ways to their lower mentality — some by bringing with them the memory of crimes unpardoned, some by bringing with them the idea of a merely animal life, others less degraded, but still in bondage to limited thought, bringing with them only the suggestion of a frivolous worldly life — in this way, by the natural operation of the Law of Suggestion, these different classes, either through remorse, or unsatisfied desires, or sheer incapacity to grasp higher principles, all remain earth-bound, suffering in exact correspondence with the nature of the suggestion they have brought along with them. The unchangeable Law is that the suggestion becomes the life; and this is equally true of suggestions of a happier sort. Those who have brought over with them the great truth that conditions are the creations of thought, and who have accustomed themselves while in objective life to dwell on good and beautiful ideas, are still able, by reason of being imbued with this suggestion, to mold the conditions of their consciousness in the subjective world in accordance with the sort of ideas which have become a second nature to them. Within the limits of these ideas the dominant suggestion to these entities is that of a Law which confers Liberty, so by using this Law of the constructive power of thought they can determine the conditions of their own consciousness; and thus instead of being compelled to suffer the nightmare dreams of the other class, they can mold their dream according to their will. We cannot conceive of such a life as theirs in the unseen as otherwise than happy, nevertheless its range is limited by the range of the conceptions they have brought with them. These may be exceedingly beautiful and thoroughly true and logical *as far as they go;* but they do not go the whole way, otherwise these spirits would not be in the category which we are considering but would belong to that still higher class who fully realize the ultimate possibilities which the Law of the Expression of Spirit provides.

The otherwise happy subjective life of these more enlightened souls has this radical defect that they have failed to bring over with them that power of original selection and initiative without which further progress is impossible. I wish the student to grasp this point very clearly, for it is of the utmost importance. Of course the basis of our further evolution is conformity to the harmonious nature of the Originating Spirit; but upon this foundation we each have to build up the superstructure of our own individuality, and every step of advance depends on our personal development of power to take that step. This is what is meant by taking an initiative. It is making a New Departure, not merely recombining the old things into fresh groupings still subject to the old laws, but introducing an entirely new element which will bring its own New Law along with it.

Now if this is the true meaning of " initiative " then that is just the power which these otherwise happy souls do not possess. For by the very conditions of the case they are living only in their subjective consciousness, and consequently are living by the law of subjective mind; and one of the chief characteristics of subjective mind is its incapacity to reason inductively, and therefore its inability to make the selection and take the initiative necessary to inaugurate a New Departure. The well established facts of mental law show conclusively that subjective mind argues only deductively. It argues quite correctly from any given premises, but it cannot take the initiative in selecting the premises — that is the province of inductive reasoning which is essentially the function of the objective mind. But by the law of Auto-suggestion this discarnate individual has brought over his premises with him, which premises are the sum-total of his inductions made during objective life, the conception of things which he held at the time he passed over, for this constituted his idea of Truth. Now he cannot add to these inductions, for he has parted with his instrument for inductive reasoning, and therefore his deductive reasoning in the purely subjective state which he has now entered is necessarily limited to the consequences which may be deducted from the premises which he has brought along with him.

In the case of the highly-developed individualities we are now considering the premises thus brought over are of a very far-reaching and beautiful character, and consequently the range of their subjective life is correspondingly wide and beautiful; but, nevertheless, it is subject to the radical defect that it is debarred from further progress for the simple reason that the individual has not brought over with him the mental faculty which can impress his subjective entity with the requisite forward movement for making a new departure into a New Order. And moreover, the higher the subjective development with which the individual passed over the more likely he will be to realize this defect. If during earth-life he had gained sufficient knowledge of these things he will carry with him the knowledge that his discarnate existence is purely subjective; and therefore he will realize that, however he may be able to order the pictures of his dream, yet it is still but a dream, and in common with all other dreams lacks the basis of solidity from which to take *really creative action.*

He knows also that the condition of other discarnate individualities is similar to his own, and that consequently each one must necessarily live in a world apart — a world of his own creation, because none of them possess the objective mentality by which to direct their subjective currents so as to make them penetrate into the sphere of another subjective entity, which is the *modus operandi* of telepathy. Thus he is conscious of his own inability to hold intercourse with other personalities; for though he may for his own pleasure create the semblance of them in his dream-life, yet he knows that these are creations of his own mind, and that while he appears to be conversing with a friend amid the most lovely surroundings the friend himself may be having experiences of a very different description. I am, of course, speaking now of persons who have passed over in a very high state of development and with a very considerable, though still imperfect, knowledge of the Law of their own being. Probably the majority take their dream-life for an external reality; and, in any case, all who have passed over without carrying their objective mentality along with them must be shut up in their individual subjective spheres and cease to function as centers of creative power so long as they do not emerge from that state.

But the highly advanced individuals of whom I am now speaking have passed over with a true knowledge of the Law of the relation between subjective and objective mind and have therefore brought with them a *subjective* knowledge of this truth; and therefore, however otherwise in a certain sense happy, they must still be conscious of a fundamental limitation which prevents their further advance. And this consciousness can produce only one result, an ever-growing longing for the removal of this limitation — and this represents the intense desire of the Spirit, as individualized in these souls, to attain to the conditions under which it can freely exercise its creative power. Sub-consciously this is the desire of *all* souls, for it is that continual pressing forward of the Spirit for manifestation out of which the whole Creative Process arises; and so it is that the great cry perpetually ascends to God from all as yet undelivered souls, whether in or out of the body, for the deliverance which they knowingly or unknowingly desire.

All this comes out of the well-ascertained facts of the law of relation between subjective and objective mind. Then comes the question, Is there no way of getting out of this law?

The answer is that we can never get away from universal principles — *but we can specialize them*. We may take it as an axiom that any law which appears to limit us contains in itself the principle by which that limitation can be overcome, just as in the case of the flotation of iron. In this axiom, then, we shall find the clue which will bring us out of the labyrinth. The same law which places various degrees of limitation upon the souls that have passed into the invisible can be so applied as to set them free. We have seen that everything turns on the obligation of our subjective part to act within the limits of the suggestion which has been most deeply impressed upon it. Then why not impress upon it the suggestion that in passing over to the other side it has brought its objective mentality along with it?

If such a suggestion were effectively impressed upon our subjective mind, then by the fundamental law of our nature our subjective mind would act in strict accordance with this suggestion, with the result that the objective mind would no longer be separated from it, and that we should carry with us into the unseen our *whole* mentality, both subjective and objective, and so be able to exercise our inductive powers of selection and initiative as well there as here.

Why not? The answer is that we cannot accept any suggestion unless we believe it to be true, and to believe it to be true we must feel that we have a solid foundation for our belief. If, then, we can find a sufficient foundation for adequately impressing this suggestion upon ourselves, then the principles of mental law assure us that we shall carry our objective faculty of initiative and selection into the unseen. Therefore our quest is to find this Foundation. Then, since we cannot accept as true what we believe to be contrary to the ultimate law of the universe, if we are to find such a foundation at all it must be within that Law; and it is for this reason that I have laid so much stress upon the Normal Standard of Human Individuality. When we are convinced that this ideal completeness is quite normal, and is a spiritual fact, not dependent upon the body, but able to control the body, then we have got the solid basis on which to carry our objective personality along with us into the unseen, and the well-established laws of our mental constitution justify the belief that we can do so.

From these considerations it is obvious that

those who thus pass over in possession of their complete mentality must be in a very different position from those who pass into a condition of merely subjective life, for they have brought their powers of selection and initiative with them, and can therefore employ their experiences in the unseen as a starting-point for still further development. So, then, the question arises, What lines will this further development be likely to follow?

We are now considering the case of persons who have reached a very high degree of development; who have succeeded in so completely uniting the subjective and objective portions of their spiritual being into a perfect whole that they can never again be severed; and who are therefore able to function with their whole consciousness on the spiritual plane. Such persons will doubtless be well aware that they have attained this degree of development by the Law of the Creative Process working in terms of their own individuality, and so they would naturally always refer to the original Cosmic Creation as the demonstration of the principle which they have to specialize for their own further evolution. Then they would find that the principle involved is that of the manifestation of Spirit in Form; and they would further see that this manifestation is not an illusion but a reality, for the simple reason that both mind and matter are equally projections from the Great Originating Spirit. Both alike are thoughts of the Divine Mind, and it is impossible to conceive any greater reality than the Divine Thought, or to get at any more substantial source of reality than that. Even if we were to picture the Divine Mind as laughing at its productions as being mere illusions *relatively to itself* (which I certainly do not), still the relation between the individual mind and material existence would be a reality for the individual, on the simple mathematical ground that like signs multiplied together invariably produce a positive result, even though the signs themselves be negative; so that, for us, at every stage of our existence substance must always be as much a reality as mind. Therefore the manifestation of Spirit in Form is the eternal principle of the Creative Process whether in the evolution of a world-system or in that of an individual.

But when we realize that by the nature of the Creative Process substance must be an eternal verity we must not suppose that this is true also of *particular forms* or of *particular modes* of matter. Substance is a necessity for the expression of Spirit, but it does not follow that Spirit is tied down to any particular mode of expression. If you fold a piece of paper into the form of a dart it will fly through the air by the law of the form which you have given it. Again, if you take the same bit of paper and fold it into the shape of a boat it will float on water by the law of the new form that you have given it. The thing formed will act in accordance with the form given it, and the same paper can be folded into different forms; but if there were no paper you could put it into any shape at all. The dart and the boat are both real so long as you retain the paper in either of those shapes; but this does not alter the fact that you can change the shapes, though your power to do so depends on the existence of the paper. This is a rough analogy of the relation between ultimate substance and particular forms, and shows us that neither substance nor shape is an illusion; both are essential to the manifestation of Spirit, only by the nature of the Creative Process the Spirit has power to determine what shape substance shall take at any particular time.

Accordingly we find the great Law that, as Spirit is the Alpha of the Creative Process, so solid material Form is its Omega; in other words the Creative Series is incomplete until solid material form is reached. Anything short of this is a condition of incompleteness, and therefore the enlightened souls who have passed over in possession of both sides of their mentality will realize that their condition, however beatific, is still one of incompleteness; and that what is wanted for completion is expression through a material body. This, then, is the direction in which such souls would use their powers of initiative and selection as being the true line of evolution—in a word they would realize that the principle of Creative Progression, when it reaches the level of fully developed mental man, necessarily implies the Resurrection of the Body, and that anything short of this would be retrogression and not progress.

At the same time persons who had passed over with this knowledge would never suppose that Resurrection meant merely the resuscitation of the old body under the old conditions; for they would see that the same inherent law which makes expression in concrete substance the ultimate of the creative series also makes this ultimate form depend on the originating movement of the spirit which produces it, and therefore that, although *some* concrete form is essential for complete manifestation, and is a substantial reality so long as it is maintained, yet the maintaining of the particular form is entirely dependent on the action of the spirit of which the form is the external clothing. This resurrection body would therefore be no mere illusory spirit-shape, yet it would not be subject to the limitations of matter as we now know it: it would be physical matter still, but entirely subject to the will of the indwelling spirit, which would not regard the denser atomic relations of the body but only its absolute and essential nature as Primary Substance. I want the student to grasp the idea that the same thing may be very different when looked at, so to say, from opposite ends of the stick. What is solid molecular matter when viewed from the outside is plastic primary substance when viewed from the inside. The relations of this new body to any stimulus proceeding from outside would be those of the external laws of Nature; but its relation to the spiritual ego working from within would be that of a plastic substance to be molded at will. The employment of such power would, however, at all times be based upon the reverent worship of the All-creating Spirit; and it would therefore never be exercised otherwise than in accordance with the harmonious progress of the Creative Process. Proceeding on these lines the spirit in the individual would stand in precisely the same relation to his body that the All-originating Spirit does to the cosmos.

This, then, is the sort of body which the instructed would contemplate as that in which he was to attain resurrection. He would regard it, not as an illusion, but as a great reality; while at the same time he would not need to trouble himself about its particular form, for he would know that it would be the perfect expression of his own conception of himself. He would know this because it is in accordance with the fundamental principle that external creation has its root in the Self-contemplation of Spirit.

Those passing over with this knowledge would obviously be in a very different position from those who passed over with only a subjective consciousness. They would bring with them powers of selection and initiative by which they could continue to impress fresh and expanding conceptions upon their subjective mind, and so cause it to carry on its work as the seed-ground of the whole individuality, instead of being shut up in itself as a mere circulus for the repetition of previously received ideas; and so in their recognition of the *principle* of physical resurrection they would have a clear and definite line of auto-suggestion. And because this suggestion is derived from the undeniable facts of the whole cosmic creation, it is one which both subjective and objective mind can accept as an established fact, and so the suggestion becomes effective. This suggestion, then, becomes the self-contemplation of the individual spirit; and because it is in strict conformity with the generic principle of the Original Creative Activity, of which the individual mind is itself a product, this becomes also the Self-contemplation of the Originating Spirit as seeing itself reflected in the individual spirit; so that, by the basic law of the Creative Process, this suggestion is bound sooner or later to work out into its corresponding fact, namely, the production of a material body free from the power of death and from all those limitations which we now associate with our physical organism.

This, then, is the hope of those who pass over in recognition of the great truth. But how about those who have passed over without that recognition? We have seen that their purely subjective condition precludes them from taking any initiative on their own account, for that requires the presence of objective mind. Their subjective mind, however, still retains its essential nature; that is, it is still susceptible to suggestion, and still possesses its inherent creativeness in working out any suggestion that is sufficiently deeply implanted in it. Here, then, opens up a vast field of activity for that other class who have passed over in possession of both sides of their mentality. By means of their powers of initiative and selection they can on the principle of telepathy cause their own subjective mind to penetrate the subjective spheres of those who do not possess those powers, and they can thus endeavor to impress upon them the great truth of the physical ultimate of the Creative Process — the truth that any series which stops short of that ultimate is incomplete, and, if insisted upon as being ultimate, must become self-destructive because in opposition to the inherent working of the Universal Creative Spirit. Then, as the perception of the true nature of the Creative Process dawned upon any subjective entity, it would by reason of accepting this suggestion begin to develop an objective mentality, and so would gradually attain to the same status as those who had passed over in full possession of all their mental powers.

But the more the objective mentality became developed in these discarnate personalities the more the need of a corresponding physical instrument would assert itself, both from their intellectual perception of the original cosmic process, and also from the inherent energy of the Spirit as centered in the ultimate ego of the individual. Not to seek material manifestation would be the contrary of all we have traced out regarding the nature of the Creative Process; and hence the law of tendency resulting from the conscious union of subjective and objective mind in the individual must necessarily be toward the production of a physical form. Only we must recollect, as I have already pointed out, that this concentration of these minds would be upon a principle

and not upon a particular bodily shape.   The
particular form they would be content to leave
to the inherent self-expressiveness of the Universal Spirit working through the particular
ego, with the result that their expectation
would be fixed upon a *general principle* of
physical Resurrection which would provide a
form suited to be the material instrument of
the highest ideal of man as a spiritual and
mental being.   Then, since the subjective mind
is the automatic builder of the body, the result
of the individual's acceptance of the Resurrection principle must be that this mental conception will eventually work out as a corresponding fact.   Whether on this planet or on some
other, matters not, for, as we have already
seen, the physical body evolved by a soul that
is conscious of its unity with the Universal
Spirit is bound to be in conformity with the
physical laws of *any* planet, though from the
standpoint of the conscious ego not limited by
them.

In this way we may conceive that those who
have passed over in possession of both sides of
their spiritual nature would find a glorious
field of usefulness in the unseen in helping to
emancipate those who had passed over in

possession of their subjective side only. But from our present analysis it will be seen that this can only be effected on the basis of a recognition of the principle of the Resurrection of the Body. Apart from the recognition of this principle the only possible conception which the discarnate individual could form of himself would be that of a purely subjective being; and this carries with it all the limitations of a subjective life unbalanced by an objective one; and so long as the principle of physical resurrection is denied, so long the life must continue to be merely subjective and consequently unprogressive.[1]

But it may be asked why those who have realized this great principle sufficiently to carry their objective mentality into the unseen state are liable to the change which we call death. The answer is that though they have realized *the general principle* they have not yet divested themselves of certain conceptions by which

[1] This view, it may be remarked, is not necessarily incompatible with the conception of reincarnation, on which theory the final resurrection or transmutation of the body would terminate the series of successive lives and deaths, thus bringing the individual out of the circle of generation, which is the circle of Karma. I may, perhaps, have the opportunity of considering this subject on some future occasion.

they limit it, and consequently by the law of subjective mind they carry those limitations into the working of the Resurrection principle itself.

They are limited by the race-belief that physical death is under all conditions a necessary law of Nature, or by the theological belief that death is the will of God; so then the question is whether these beliefs are well founded. Of course appeal is made to universal experience, but it does not follow that the universal experience of the past is bound to be the universal experience of the future — the universal experience of the past was that no man had ever flown across the English Channel, yet now it has been done. What we have to do, therefore, is not to bother about past experience, but to examine the inherent nature of the Law of Life and see whether it does not contain possibilities of further development. And the first step in this direction is to see whether what we have hitherto considered limitations of the law are really integral parts of the law itself. The very statement of this question shows the correct answer; for how can a force acting in one direction be an integral part of a force acting in the opposite direction? How can the force which pulls a thing down be an integral part of the force which builds it up? To suppose, therefore, that the limitations of the law are an integral portion of the law itself is a *reductio ad absurdum*.

For these reasons the argument from the past experience of the race counts for nothing; and when we examine the theological argument we shall find that it is only the old argument from past experience in another dress. It is alleged that death is the will of God. How do we know that it is the will of God? Because the facts prove it so, is the ultimate answer of all religious systems with one exception; so here we are back again at the old race-experience as the criterion of truth. Therefore the theological argument is nothing but the materialistic argument disguised. It is in our more or less conscious acceptance of the materialistic argument, under any of its many disguises, that the limitation of life is to be found — not in the Law of Life itself; and if we are to bring into manifestation the infinite possibilities latent in that Law it can only be by looking steadily into the *principle* of the Law and resolutely denying everything that opposes it. The Principle of Life must of necessity be Affirmative, and affirmative throughout, without any negative anywhere — if we once realize this we shall be able to un- mask the enemy and silence his guns.

Now to do this is precisely the one object of the Bible; and it does it in a thoroughly logical manner, always leading on to the ultimate result by successive links of cause and effect. People will tell you that the Bible is their authority for saying that Death is the will of God; but these are people who read it carelessly; and ultimately the only reason they can give you for their manner of interpreting the Bible is that the facts prove their interpre- tation to be correct; so that in the last resort you will always find you have got back to the old materialistic argument from past race- experience, which logically proves nothing. These are good well-meaning people with a limited idea which they read into the Bible, and so limit its promises by making physical death an essential preliminary to Resurrection. They grasp, of course, the great central idea that Perfected Man possesses a joyous im- mortal Life permeating spirit, soul and body; but they relegate it to some dim and distant future, entirely disconnected from the present law of our being, not seeing that if we are to have eternal life it must necessarily be involved in some principle which is eternal, and therefore existing, at any rate latently, at the present moment. Hence, though their fundamental principle is true, they are all the time mentally limiting it, with the result that they themselves create the conditions they impose upon it, and consequently the principle will work (as principles always do) in accordance with the conditions provided for its action.

Unless, therefore, this limiting belief is entirely eradicated, the individual, though realizing the fundamental principle of Life, is bound to pass out of physical existence; but on the other hand, since he does take the recognition of this fundamental principle with him, it is bound to bear fruit sooner or later in a joyous Resurrection, while the intermediate state can only be a peaceful anticipation of that supreme event. This is the answer to the question why those who have realized the great principle sufficiently to carry their objective mentality into the unseen world are still liable to physical death; and in the last analysis it will be found to resolve itself into the remains of race-belief based upon past experience. These are they who pass over in sure and certain hope of a glorious Resurrection — sure and certain because founded upon the very Being of God Himself, that inherent Life of the All-creating Divine Spirit which is the perpetual interaction of the Eternal Love and Beauty. They have grasped the Life-giving Truth, only they have postponed its operation, because they have the fixed idea that its present fruition is an absolute impossibility.

But if we ask the reason for this idea it always comes back to the old materialistic argument from the experience of past conditions, while the whole nature of advance is in the opening up of new conditions. And in this advance the Bible is the pioneer book. Its whole purport is to tell us most emphatically that death is *not* the will of God. In the story of Eden God is represented as warning man of the poisonous nature of the forbidden fruit, which is incompatible with the idea of death as an essential feature of man's nature. Then from the point where man has taken the poison all the rest of the Bible is devoted to telling us how to get rid of it. Christ, it tells us, was manifested to bring Life and Immortality to light — to abolish death — to destroy the works of the devil, that is the death-dealing power, for " he that hath the power of death is the devil." It is impossible to reconcile this life-giving conception of the Bible with the idea that death at any stage or in any degree is the desire of God. Let us, therefore, start with the recognition that this negative force, whether in its minor degrees as disease or in its culmination as death, is that which it is the will of God to abolish. This also is logical; for if God be the Universal Spirit of Life finding manifestation in individual lives, how can the desire of this Spirit be to act in opposition to its own manifestation? Therefore Scripture and common-sense alike assure us that the will of God toward us is Life and not death.[1]

We may therefore start on our quest for Life with the happy certainty that God is on our side. But people will meet us with the objection that though God wills Life to us, He does not will it just yet, but only in some dim far-off future. How do we know this? Certainly not from the Bible. In the Bible

[1] See my " Bible Mystery and Bible Meaning."

Jesus speaks of two classes of persons who believe on Him as the Manifestation or Individualisation of the Spirit of Life. He speaks of those who, having passed through death, still believe on Him, and says that these *shall* live — a future event. And at the same time He speaks of those who are living and believe on Him, and says that they shall never die — thus contemplating the entire elimination of the contingency of death (John xi. 25).

Again St. Paul expresses his wish not to be unclothed but to be clothed upon, which he certainly would not have done had he considered the latter alternative a nonsensical fancy. And in another place he expressly states that we shall not all die, but that some shall be transmuted into the Resurrection body without passing through physical death. And if we turn to the Old Testament we find two instances in which this is said to have actually occurred, those of Enoch and Elijah. And we may note in passing that the Bible draws our attention to certain facts about these two personages which are important as striking at the root of the notion that austerities of some sort are necessary for the great attainment. Of Enoch we are expressly told that he was the father of a large family, and of Elijah that he was a man of like nature with ourselves — thus showing us what is wanted is not a shutting of ourselves off from ordinary human life but such a clear realization of the Universal Principle, of which our personal life is the more or less conscious manifestation, that our commonest actions will be hallowed by the Divine Presence; and so the grand dénouement will be only the natural result of our daily habit of walking with God. From the stand-point of the Bible, therefore, the attainment of physical regeneration without passing through death is not an impossibility, nor is it necessarily relegated to some far off future. Whatever any one else may say to the contrary, the Bible contemplates such a dénouement of human evolution as a present possibility.

Then if we argue from the philosophical stand-point we arrive at precisely the same result. Past experience proves nothing, and we must therefore make a fresh start by going back to the Original Creative action of the Spirit of Life itself. Then, if we take this as our starting point, remembering that at the stage of this *original* movement there can be no intervention by a second power, because there

is none, why should we mentally impose any restriction upon the action of the Creative
Power? Certainly not by its own Law of
Tendency, for that must always be toward
fuller self-expression; and since this can only
take place through the individual, the desire of
the Spirit must always be toward the increasing of the individual life. Nor yet from anything in the created substance, for that would
either be to suppose the Spirit creating something in limitation of its own Self-expression,
or else to suppose that the limiting substance
was created by some other power working
against the Spirit; and as this would mean a
Duality of powers we should not have reached
the Originating Power at all, and so we might
put Spirit and Substance equally out of court
as both being merely modes of secondary causation. But if we see that the Universal Substance must be created by emanation from the
Universal Spirit, then we see that no limitation of Spirit by substance is possible. We
may therefore feel assured that no limitation
proceeds either from the will of the Spirit or
from the nature of Substance.

Where, then, does limitation come from?
Limiting conditions are created by the same

power which creates everything else, namely, the Self-contemplation of Spirit. This is why it is so important to realize that the individual mind forms a center from which the self-contemplating action of Spirit is specialized in terms of the individual's own mode of thinking, and therefore so long as the individual contemplates negative conditions as being *of the essence* of his own personality, he is in effect employing the Creative Power of the Self-contemplation of Spirit invertedly, destructively instead of constructively. The Law of the Self-contemplation of Spirit as the Creative Power is as true in the microcosm as in the macrocosm, and so the individual's contemplation of himself as subject to the law of sin and death keeps him subject to that law, while the opposite self-contemplation, the contemplation of himself as rejoicing in the Life of the Spirit, the Perfect Law of Liberty, must necessarily produce the opposite results.

Why, then, should not regeneration be accomplished here and now? I can see no reason against it, either Scriptural or philosophical, except our own difficulty in getting rid of the race-traditions which are so deeply embedded in our subjective minds. To get rid of these we require a firm basis on which to receive the opposite suggestion. We need to be convinced that our ideal of a regenerated self is in accord with the Normal Standard of Humanity and is within the scope of the laws of the universe. Now to make clear to us the *infinitude* of the truly Normal Standard of Humanity is the whole purpose of the Bible; and the Manifestation of this Standard is set before us in the Central Personality of the Scriptures who is at once the Son of God and the Son of Man — the Great Exception, if you will, to man as we know him now, but the Exception which proves the Rule. In proportion as we begin to realize this we begin to introduce into our own life the action of that Personal Factor on which all further development depends; and when our recognition is complete we shall find that we also are children of God.

CHAPTER IX

Conclusion

WE are now in a position to see the place occupied by the individual in the Creative Order. We have found that the originating and maintaining force of the whole Creative Process is the Self-contemplation of the Spirit, and that this necessarily produces a Reciprocal corresponding to the idea embodied in the contemplation, and thus manifesting that idea in a correlative Form. We have found that in this way the externalization of the idea progresses from the condensation of the primary nebula to the production of human beings as a race, and that at this point the simple *generic* reproduction of the idea terminates. This means that up to, and including, *genus homo,* the individual, whether plant, animal, or man, is what it is simply by reason of race conditions and not by exercise of deliberate choice. Then we have seen that the next step in advance must

128

necessarily be by the individual becoming aware that he has power to mold the conditions of his own consciousness and environment by the creative power of his thought; thus not only enabling him to take a conscious part in his own further evolution but precluding him from evolving any further except by the right exercise of this power; and we have found that the crux of the passage from the Fourth to the Fifth Kingdom is to get people so to understand the nature of their creative power as not to use it destructively. Now what we require to see is that the Creative Process has always only one way of working, and that is by Reciprocity or Reflection, or, as we might say, by the law of Action and Re-action, the re-action being always equivalent and correspondent to the action which generated it. If this Law of Reciprocity be grasped then we see how the progress of the Creative Process must at length result in producing a being who himself possesses the power of independent spiritual initiative and is thus able to carry on the creative work from the stand-point of his own individuality.

Now the great crux is first to get people to see that they possess this power at all, and then to get them to use it in the right direction. When our eyes begin to open to the truth that we do possess this power the temptation is to ignore the fact that our power of initiative is itself a product of the similar power subsisting in the All-originating Spirit. If this origin of our own creative faculty is left out of sight we shall fail to recognize the Livingness of the Greater Life within which we live. We shall never get nearer to it than what we may call its *generic* level, the stage at which the Creative Power is careful of the type or race but is careless of the individual; and so at this level we shall never pass into the Fifth Kingdom which is the Kingdom of Individuality — we have missed the whole point of the transition to the more advanced mode of being, in which the individual consciously functions as a creative center, because we have no conception of a Universal Power that works at any higher level than the generic, and consequently to reach a specific personal exercise of creative power we should have to conceive of ourselves as transcending the Universal Law. But if we realize that our own power of creative initiative has its origin in the similar faculty of the All-Originating Mind then we see that the way to maintain the Life-giving energy in ourselves is to use our power of spiritual initiative so as to impress upon the Spirit the conception of ourselves as standing related to It in a specific, individual, and personal way that takes us out of the mere category of *genus homo* and gives us a specific spiritual individuality of our own. Thus our mental action produces a corresponding re-action in the mind of the Spirit, which in its turn reproduces itself as a special manifestation of the Life of the Spirit in us; and so long as this circulation between the individual spirit and the Great Spirit is kept up, the individual life will be maintained, and will also strengthen as the circulation continues, for the reason that the Spirit, as the Original Creative Power, is a Multiplying Force, and the current sent into it is returned multiplied, just as in telegraphy the feeble current received from a distance at the end of a long line operates to start a powerful battery in the receiving office, which so multiplies the force as to give out a clear message, which but for the multiplication of the original movement could not have been done. Something like this we may picture the multiplying tendency of the Originating Mind, and consequently the longer the circulation between it and the individual mind goes on the stronger the latter becomes; and this process growing habitual becomes at last automatic, thus producing an endless flow of Life continually expanding in intelligence, love, power and joy.

But we must note carefully that all this can only proceed from the individual's recognition that his own powers are a derivative from the All-originating Spirit, and that they can continue to be used constructively only so long as they are employed in harmony with the inherent Forward Movement of the Spirit. Therefore to insure this eternally flowing stream of Life from the Universal Spirit into the individual there must be *no inversion* in the individual's presentation of himself to the Originating Power: for through the very same Law by which we seek Life — the Life namely, of reciprocal action and re-action — every inversion we bring with us in presenting ourselves to the Spirit is bound to be faithfully reproduced in a corresponding re-action, thus adulterating the stream of Pure Life, and rendering it less life-giving in proportion to the extent to which we invert the action of the Life-principle; so that in extreme cases the stream flowing through and from the individual may be rendered absolutely poisonous and deadly, and the more so the greater his recognition of his own personal power to employ spiritual forces.

The existence of these negative possibilities in the spiritual world should never be overlooked, and therefore the essential condition for receiving the Perfect Fulness of Life is that we should present ourselves before the Eternal Spirit free from every trace of inversion. To do this means to present ourselves in the likeness of the Divine Ideal; and in this self-presentation the initiative, so far as the individual is consciously concerned, must necessarily be taken by himself. He is to project into the Eternal Mind the conception of himself as identical with its Eternal Ideal; and if he can do this, then by the Law of the Creative Process a return current will flow from the Eternal Mind reproducing this image in the individual with a continually growing power. Then the question is, How are we to do this?

The answer is that to take the initiative for inducing this flow of Life individually it is a *sine qua non* that the conditions enabling us to do so should first be presented to us universally.

This is in accordance with the general principle that we can never create a force but can only specialize it. Only here the power we are wanting to specialize is the very Power of Specialization itself; and therefore, paradoxical as it may seem, what we require to have shown us is the Universality of Specialization.

Now this is what the Bible puts before us in its central figure. Taking the Bible statements simply and literally they show us this unique Personality as the Principle of Humanity, alike in its spiritual origin and its material manifestation, carried to the logical extreme of specialization; while at the same time, as the embodiment of the original polarity of Spirit and Substance, this Personality, however unique, is absolutely universal; so that the Bible sets Jesus Christ before us as the answer to the philosophic problem of how to specialize the universal, while at the same time preserving its universality.

If, then, we fix our thought upon this unique Personality as the embodiment of *universal* principles, it follows that those principles must exist in ourselves also, and that His actual specialization of them is the earnest of our potential specialization of them. Then if we fix our thought on this potential in ourselves as being identical with its manifestation in Him, we can logically claim our identity with Him, so that what He has done we have done, what He is, we are, and thus recognizing ourselves in Him we present *this* image of ourselves to the Eternal Mind, with the result that we bring with us no inversion, and so import no negative current into our stream of Life.

Thus it is that we reach "the Father" through "the Son," and that He is able to keep us from falling and to present us faultless before the presence of the Divine glory with exceeding joy (Jude 24). The Gospel of "the Word made flesh" is not the meaningless cant of some petty sect nor yet the cunning device of priestcraft, though it has been distorted in both these directions; but it can give a reason for itself, and is founded upon the deepest laws of the threefold constitution of man, embracing the *whole* man, body, soul and spirit. It is not opposed to Science but is the culmination of all science whether physical or mental. It is philosophical and logical throughout if you start the Creative Process where alone it can start, in the Self-contemplation of the Spirit. The more carefully we examine into the claims of the Gospel of Christ the more we shall find all the current objections to it melt away and disclose their own superficialness. We shall find that Christ is indeed the Mediator between God and Man, not by the arbitrary fiat of a capricious Deity, but by a logical law of sequence which solves the problem of making extremes meet, so that the Son of Man is also the Son of God; and when we see the reason why this is so we thereby receive power to become ourselves sons of God, which is the dénouement of the Creative Process in the Individual.

These closing lines are not the place to enter upon so great a subject, but I hope to follow it up in another volume and to show in detail the logic of the Bible teaching, what it saves us from and what it leads us to; to show while giving due weight to the value of other systems how it differs from them and transcends them; to glance, perhaps, for a moment at the indications of the future and to touch upon some of the dangers of the present and the way to escape from them. Nor would I pass over in silence another and important aspect of the Gospel contained in Christ's commission to His followers to heal the sick. This also follows logically from the Law of the Creative Process if we trace carefully the sequence of connections from the indwelling Ego to the outermost of its vehicles; while the effect of the recognition of these great truths upon the individuality that has for a time put off its robe of flesh, opens out a subject of paramount interest. Thus it is that on every plane Christ is the Fulfilling of the Law, and that " Salvation " is not a silly shiboleth but the logical and vital process of our advance into the unfoldment of the next stage of the limitless capacities of our being. Of these things I hope to write in another volume, should it be permitted to me, and in the meanwhile I would commend the present abstract statement of principles to the reader's attention in the hope that it may throw some light on the fundamental nature of these momentous questions. The great thing to bear in mind is that if a thing is true at all there must be a reason why it is true, and when we come to see this reason we know the truth at first hand for ourselves and not from some one else's report — then it becomes really our own and we begin to learn how to use it. This is the secret of the individual's progress in any art, science, or business, and the same method will serve equally well in our search after Life itself, and as we thus follow up the great quest we shall find that on every plane the Way, the Truth, and the Life are ONE.

"A little philosophy inclineth a man's mind to atheism, but depth in philosophy bringeth men's minds about to religion."—*Bacon. Essay xvi.*

CHAPTER X

THE DIVINE OFFERING

I TAKE the present opportunity of a new edition to add a few pages on certain points which appear to me of vital importance, and the connection of which with the preceding chapters will, I hope, become evident as the reader proceeds. Assuming the existence in each individual of a creative power of thought which, in relation to himself, reflects the same power existing in the Universal Mind, our right employment of this power becomes a matter of extreme moment to ourselves. Its inverted use necessarily holds us fast in the bondage from which we are seeking to escape, and equally necessarily its right use brings us into Liberty; and therefore if any Divine revelation exists at all its purpose must be to lead us away from the inverted use of our creative faculty and into such a higher specializing of it as will produce the desired result. Now the purpose of the Bible is to do this, and it seeks to effect this work by a dual operation. It places before us that Divine Ideal of which I have already spoken, and at the same time bases this ideal upon the recognition of a Divine Sacrifice. These two conceptions are so intimately interwoven in Scripture that they cannot be separated, but at the present day there is a growing tendency to attempt to make this separation and to discard the conception of a Divine Sacrifice as unphilosophical, that is as having no nexus of cause and effect. What I want, therefore, to point out in these additional pages is that there is such a nexus, and that so far from being without a sequence of cause and effect it has its root in the innermost principles of our own being. It is not contrary to Law but proceeds from the very nature of the Law itself.

The current objection to the Bible teaching on this subject is that no such sacrifice could have been required by God, either because the Originating Energy can have no consciousness of Personality and is only a blind force, or because, if " God is Love," He could not demand such a sacrifice. On the former hypothesis we are of course away from the Bible teaching altogether and have nothing to do with it; but, as I have said elsewhere, the fact of our own consciousness of personality can only be accounted for by the existence, however hidden, of a corresponding quality in the Originating Spirit. Therefore I will confine my remarks to the question how Love, as the originating impulse of all creation, can demand such a sacrifice. And to my mind the answer· is that God does not demand it. It is Man who demands it. It is the instinctive craving of the human soul for *certainty* that requires a demonstration so convincing as to leave no room for doubt of our perfectly happy relation to the Supreme Spirit, and consequently to all that flows from it, whether on the side of the visible or of the invisible. When we grasp the fact that such a standpoint of certainty is the necessary foundation for the building up in ourselves of the Divine Ideal then it becomes clear that to afford us this firm basis is the greatest work that the Spirit, in its relation to human personality, could do.

We are often told that the offering of sacrifices had its origin in primitive man's conception of his gods as beings which required to be propitiated so as to induce them to do good or abstain from doing harm; and very likely this was the case. The truth at the back of this conception is the feeling that there is a higher power upon which man is dependent; and the error is in supposing that this power is limited by an individuality which can be enriched by selling its good offices, or which blackmails you by threats. In either case it wants to get something out of you, and from this it follows that its own power of supplying its own wants must be limited, otherwise it would not require to be kept in good temper by gifts. In very undeveloped minds such a conception results in the idea of numerous gods, each having, so to say, his own particular line of business; and the furthest advance this mode of thought is capable of is the reduction of these various deities to two antagonistic powers of Good and of Evil. But the result in either case is the same, so long as we start with the hypothesis that the Good will do us more good and the Evil do us less harm by reason of our sacrifices, for then it logically follows that the more valuable your sacrifices and the oftener they are presented the better chance you have of good luck. Doubtless some such conception as this was held by the mass of the Hebrew people under the sacrificial system of the

Levitical Law, and perhaps this was one reason why they were so prone to fall into idolatry — for in this view their fundamental notion was practically identical in its nature with that of the heathen around them. Of course this was not the fundamental idea embodied in the Levitical system itself. The root of that system was the symbolizing of a supreme ideal of reconciliation hereafter to be manifested in action. Now a symbol is not the thing symbolized. The purpose of a symbol is twofold, to put us upon enquiry as to the reality which it indicates, and to bring that reality to our minds by suggestion when we look at the symbol; but if it does not do this, and we rest only in the symbol, nothing will come of it, and we are left just where we were. That the symbolic nature of the Levitical sacrifice was clearly perceived by the deeper thinkers among the Hebrews is attested by many passages in the Bible —" Sacrifice and burnt offering thou wouldest not " (Psalms xl: 6, and li: 16) and other similar utterances; and the distinction between these symbols and that which they symbolized is brought out in the Epistle to the Hebrews by the argument that if those sacrifices had afforded a sufficient standpoint for the effectual realization of cleansing then the worshiper would not need to have repeated them because he would have no more consciousness of sin (Hebrews x: 2).

This brings us to the essential point of the whole matter. What we want is the certainty that there is no longer any separation between us and the Divine Spirit by reason of sin, either as overt acts of wrong doing or as error of principle; and the whole purpose of the Bible is to lead us to this assurance. Now such an assurance cannot be based on any sort of sacrifices that require repetition, for then we could never know whether we had given enough either in quality or quantity. It must be a once-for-all business or it is no use at all; and so the Bible makes the once-for-allness of the offering the essential point of its teaching. "He that has been bathed does not need to be bathed again" (John xiii: 10). "There is now no condemnation to them which are in Christ Jesus" (Romans viii: 1).

Various intellectual difficulties, however, hinder many people from seeing the working of the law of cause and effect in this presentment. One is the question, How can moral guilt be transferred from one person to another? What is called the " forensic " argument (i.e., the court of law argument) that Christ undertook to suffer in our stead as our *surety* is undoubtedly open to this objection. Suretyship must by its very nature be confined to civil obligations and cannot be extended to criminal liability, and so the " forensic " argument may be set aside as very much a legal fiction. But if we realize the Bible teaching that Christ is the Son of God, that is, the Divine Principle of Humanity out of which we originated and subsisting in us all, however unconsciously to ourselves, then we see that sinners as well as saints are included in this Principle; and consequently that the Self-offering of Christ must actually include the self-offering of every human being in the acknowledgment (however unknown to his *objective* mentality) of his sin. If we can grasp this somewhat abstract point of view it follows that in the Person of Christ every human being, past, present, and to come, was self-offered for the condemnation of his sin — a *self*-condemnation and a *self*-offering, and hence a cleansing, for the simple reason that if you can get a man to realize his past error, really see his mistake, he won't do it again; and it is the perpetuation of sin and error that has to be got rid of — to do this universally would be to regain Paradise. Seen therefore in this light there is no question of transference of moral guilt, and I take it this is St. Paul's meaning when he speaks of our being partakers in Christ's death.

Then there is the objection, How can past sins be done away with? If we accept the philosophical conclusion that Time has no substantive existence then all that remains is states of consciousness. As I have said in the earlier part of this book, the Self-Contemplation of Spirit is the cause of all our perception of existence and environment; and consequently if the Self-Contemplation of the Spirit from any center of individualization is that of entire harmony and the absence of anything that would cause any consciousness of separation, then past sins cease to have any part in this self-recognition, and consequently cease to have any place in the world of existence. The foundation of the whole creative process is the calling into Light out of Darkness —" that which makes manifest is light "— and consequently the converse action is that of sending out of Light into Darkness, that is, into Not-being. Now this is exactly what the Spirit says in the Bible —" I, even I, am He that blotteth out thy transgressions " (Isaiah xliii: 25). Blotting out is the sending out of manifestation into the darkness of non-manifestation, out of Being into Not-being; and in this way the past error ceases to have any existence and so ceases to have any further effect upon us. It is "blotted out," and from this new standpoint has never been at all; so that to continue to contemplate it is to give a false sense of existence to that which in effect has no existence. It is that Affirmation of Negation which is the root of all evil. It is the inversion of our God-given creative power of thought, calling into existence that which in the Perfect Life of the Spirit never had or could have any existence, and therefore it creates the sense of inharmony, opposition, and separation. Of course this is only relatively to ourselves, for we cannot create eternal principles. They are the Being of God; and as I have already shown these great Principles of the Affirmative may be summed up in the two words Love and Beauty — Love in essence and Beauty in manifestation; but since we can only live from the standpoint of our own consciousness we can make a false creation built upon the idea of opposites to the all-creating Love and Beauty, which false creation with all its accompaniments of limitation, sin, sorrow, sickness, and death, must necessarily be real to us until we perceive that these things were not created by God, the Spirit of the Affirmative, but by our own inversion of our true relation to the All-creating Being.

When, then, we view the matter in this light the Offering once for all of the Divine Sacrifice for the sin of the whole world is seen not to be a mere ecclesiastical dogma having no relation of cause and effect, but to be the highest application of the same principle of cause and effect by which the whole creation, ourselves included, has been brought into existence — the Self-Contemplation of Spirit producing corresponding manifestation, only now working on the level of Individual Personality.

As I have shown at the beginning of this book the cosmic manifestation of principles is not sufficient to bring out all that there is in them. To do this their action must be specialized by the introduction of the Personal Factor. They are represented by the Pillar Jachin, but it must be equilibriated by the Pillar Boaz, Law and Personality the two Pillars of the Universe; and in the One Offering we have the supreme combination of these two principles, the highest specialization of Law by the highest power of Personality. These are eternal principles, and therefore we are told that the Lamb was slain from the foundation of the world; and because "thoughts are things" this supreme manifestation of the creative interaction of Law and Personality was bound eventually to be manifested in concrete action in the world conditioned by time and space; and so it was that the supreme manifestation of the Love of God to meet the supreme need of Man took place. The history of the Jewish nation is the history of the working of the law of cause and effect, under the guidance of the Divine Wisdom, so as to provide the necessary conditions for the greatest event in the world's history; for if Christ was to appear it must be in *some* nation, in *some* place, and at *some* time: but to trace the steps by which, through an intelligible sequence of causes, these necessary conditions were provided belongs rather to an investigation of Bible history than to our present purpose, so I will not enter into these details here. But what I hope I have in some measure made clear is that there is a reason why Christ should be manifested, and should suffer, and rise again, and that so far from being a baseless superstition the Reconciling of the world to God through the One Offering once-for-all offered for the sin of the whole world, lays the immovable foundation upon which we may build securely for all the illimitable future.

CHAPTER XI

OURSELVES IN THE DIVINE OFFERING

IF we have grasped the principle I have endeavored to state in the last chapter we shall find that with this new standpoint a new life and a new world begin to open out to us. This is because we are now living from a new recognition of ourselves and of God. Eternal Truth, that which is the essential reality of Being, is *always* the same; it has never altered, for whatever is capable of passing away and giving place to something else is not eternal, and therefore the real essence of our being, as proceeding from God and subsisting in Him has always been the same. But this is the very fact which we have hitherto lost sight of; and since our perception of life is the measure of our individual consciousness of it, we have imposed upon ourselves a world of limitation, a world filled with the power of the negative, because we have viewed things from that standpoint. What takes place, therefore, when we realize the truth of our Redemption

151

is not a change in our essential relation to the Parent Spirit, the Eternal Father, but an awakening to the perception of this eternal and absolutely perfect relation. We see that in reality it has never been otherwise for the simple reason that in the very nature of Being it *could* not be otherwise; and when we see this we see also that what has hitherto been wrong has not been the working of "the Father" but our conception of the existence of some other power, a power of negation, limitation, and destructiveness, the very opposite to all that the Creative Spirit, by the very fact of Its Creativeness, must be. That wonderful parable of the Prodigal Son shows us that he never ceased to be a son. It was not his Father who sent him away from home but his notion that he could do better "on his own," and we all know what came of it. But when he returned to the Father he found that from the Father's point of view he had never been otherwise than a son, and that all the trouble he had gone through was not "of the Father" but was the result of his own failure to realize what the Father and the Home really were.[1]

[1] See "Bible Mystery and Bible Meaning" by the present author.

Now this is exactly the case with ourselves. When we wake up to the truth we find that, so far as the Father is concerned, we have always been in Him and in His home, for we are made in His image and likeness and are reflections of His own Being. He says to us " Son, thou art ever with me and all that I have is thine." The Self-Contemplation of Spirit is the Creative Power creating an environment corresponding to the mode of consciousness contemplated, and therefore in proportion as we contemplate ourselves as centers of individualization for the Divine Spirit we find ourselves surrounded by a new environment reflecting the harmonious conditions which pre-exist in the Thought of the Spirit.

This, then, is the sequence of Cause and Effect involved in the teaching of the Bible. Man is *in essence* a spiritual being, the reflection on the plane of individual personality of that which the All-Originating Spirit is in Itself, and is thus in that reciprocal relation to the Spirit which is Love. This is the first statement of his creation in Genesis — God saw all that He had made and behold it was very good, Man included. Then the Fall is the failure of the lower mentality to realize that

God IS Love, in a word that Love is the only ultimate Motive Power it is possible to conceive, and that the creations of Love cannot be otherwise than good and beautiful. The lower mentality conceives an opposite quality of Evil and thus produces a motive power the opposite of Love, which is Fear; and so Fear is born into the world giving rise to the whole brood of evil, anger, hatred, envy, lies, violence, and the like, and on the external plane giving rise to discordant vibrations which are the root of physical ill. If we analyze our motives we shall find that they are always some mode either of Love or Fear; and fear has its root in the recognition of some power other than Perfect Love, which is God the ONE all-embracing Good. Fear has a creative force which invertedly mimics that of Love; but the difference between them is that Love is eternal and Fear is not. Love as the Original Creative Motive is the only logical conclusion we can come to as to why we ourselves or any other creation exists. Fear is illogical because to regard it as having any place in the Orignal Creative Motive involves a contradiction in terms.

By accepting the notion of a dual power,

that of Good *and* Evil, the inverted creative
working of Fear is introduced with all its attendant train of evil things.   This is the eating
of the deadly tree which occasions the Fall,
and therefore the Redemption which requires
to be accomplished is a redemption from Fear
— not merely from this or that particular fear
but from the very Root of Fear, which root
is unbelief in the Love of God, the refusal to
believe that Love alone is the Creating Power
in all things, whether small beyond our recognition or great beyond our conception.   Therefore to bring about this Redemption there must
be such a manifestation of the Divine Love
to Man as, when rightly apprehended, will leave
no ground for fear; and when we see that the
Sacrifice of the Cross was the Self-Offering of
Love made in order to provide this manifestation, then we see that all the links in the chain
of Cause and Effect are complete, and that
Fear never had any place in the Creative Principle, whether as acting in the creation of a
world or of a man.   The root, therefore, of
all the trouble of the world consists in the
Affirmation of Negation, in using our creative
power of thought invertedly, and thus giving
substance to that which *as principle* has no

existence. So long as this negative action of thought continues so long will it produce its natural effect; whether in the individual or in the mass. The experience is perfectly real while it lasts. Its unreality consists in the fact that there was never any real need for it; and the more we grasp the truth of the all-embracingness of the ONE Good, both as Cause and as Effect, on all planes, the more the experience of its opposite will cease to have any place in our lives.

This truly New Thought puts us in an entirely new relation to the whole of our environment, opening out possibilities hitherto undreamt of, and this by an orderly sequence of law which is naturally involved in our new mental attitude; but before considering the prospect thus offered it is well to be quite clear as to what this new mental attitude really is; for it is our adoption of this attitude that is the Key to the whole position. Put briefly it is ceasing to include the idea of limitations in our conception of the working of the All-Creating Spirit. Here are some specimens of the way in which we limit the creative working of the Spirit. We say, I am too old now to start this or that new sort of work. This is to deny the power of the Spirit to vivify our physical or mental faculties, which is illogical if we consider that it is the same Spirit that brought us into any existence at all. It is like saying that when a lamp is beginning to burn low the same person who first filled it with oil cannot replenish it and make it burn brightly again. Or we say, I cannot do so and so because I have not the means. When you were fourteen did you know where all the means were coming from which were going to support you till now when you are perhaps forty or fifty? So you should argue that the same power that has worked in the past can continue to work in the future. If you say the means came in the past quite naturally through ordinary channels, that is no objection; on the contrary the more reason for saying that suitable channels will open in the future. Do you expect God to put cash into your desk by a conjuring trick? Means come through recognizable channels, that is to say we recognize the channels by the fact of the stream flowing through them; and one of our most common mistakes is in thinking that we ourselves have to fix the particular channel beforehand. We say in effect that the Spirit cannot open other channels, and so we stop them up. Or we say, our past experience speaks to the contrary, thus assuming that our past experiences have included all possibilities and have exhausted the laws of the universe, an assumption which is negatived by every fresh discovery even in physical science. And so we go on limiting the power of the Spirit in a hundred different ways.

But careful consideration will show that, though the modes in which we limit it are as numerous as the circumstances with which we have to deal, the thing with which we limit it is always the same — it is by the introduction of our own personality. This may appear at first a direct contradiction of all that I have said about the necessity for the Personal Factor, but it is not. Here is a paradox.

To open out into manifestation the wonderful possibilities hidden in the Creative Power of the Universe we require to do two things — to see that we ourselves are necessary as centers for focussing that power, and at the same time to withdraw the thought of ourselves as contributing anything to its efficiency. It is not I that work but the Power; yet the Power needs me because it cannot specialize itself without me — in a word each is the complementary of the other: and the higher the degree of specialization is to be the more necessary is the intelligent and willing co-operation of the individual.

This is the Scriptural paradox that "the son can do nothing of himself," and yet we are told to be "fellow-workers with God." It ceases to be a paradox, however, when we realize the relation between the two factors concerned, God and Man. Our mistake is in not discriminating between their respective functions, and putting Man in the place of God. In our everyday life we do this by measuring the power of God by our past experiences and the deductions we draw from them; but there is another way of putting Man in the place of God, and that is by the misconception that the All-Originating Spirit is merely a cosmic force without intelligence, and that Man has to originate the intelligence without which no specific purpose can be conceived. This latter is the error of much of the present day philosophy and has to be specially guarded against. This was perceived by some of the medieval students of these things, and they accordingly distinguished between what they called Animus Dei and Anima Mundi, the Divine Spirit and

the Soul of the Universe.   Now the distinction
is this, that the essential quality of Animus Dei
is Personality — not A Person, but the very
Principle of Personality itself — while the essential quality of Anima Mundi is Impersonal-
ity.   Then right here comes in that importance
of the Personal Factor of which I have already
spoken.   The powers latent in the Impersonal
are brought out to their fullest development
by the operation of the Personal.   This of
course does not consist in changing the nature
of those powers, for that is impossible, but in
making such combinations of them by Personal
Selection as to produce results which could not
otherwise be obtained.   Thus, for example,
Number is in itself impersonal and no one can
alter the laws which are inherent in it; but
what we can do is to select particular numbers
and the sort of relation, such as subtraction,
multiplication, etc., which we will establish between them; and then by the inherent Law of
Number a certain result is bound to work out.
Now our own essential quality is the consciousness of Personality; and as we grow into the
recognition of the fact that the Impersonal is,
as it were, crying out for the operation upon
it of the Personal in order to bring its latent

powers into working, we shall see how limitless is the field that thus opens before us.

The prospect is wonderful beyond our present conception, and full of increasing glory if we realize the true foundation on which it rests. But herein lies the danger. It consists in not realizing that the Infinite of the Impersonal *is* and also that the Infinite of the Personal *is*. Both are Infinite and so require differentiation through our own personality, but in their essential quality each is the exact balance of the other — not in contradiction to each other, but as complementary to one another, each supplying what the other needs for its full expression, so that the two together make a perfect whole. If, however, we see this relation and our own position as the connecting link between them, we shall see only ourselves as the Personal Factor; but the more we realize, both by theory and experience, the power of human personality brought into contact with the Impersonal Soul of Nature, and employed with a Knowledge of its power and a corresponding exercise of the will, the less we shall be inclined to regard ourselves as the supreme factor in the chain of cause and effect. Consideration of this argument points to the

danger of much of the present day teaching regarding the exercise of Thought Power as a
creative agency. The principle on which this
teaching is based is sound and legitimate for it
is inherent in the nature of things; but the error is in supposing that we ourselves are the
ultimate source of Personality instead of
merely the distributors and specializers of it.
The logical result of such a mental attitude is
that putting ourselves in the place of all that
is worshiped as God which is spoken of in the
second chapter of the Second Epistle to the
Thessalonians and other parts of Scripture.
By the very hypothesis of the case we then
know no higher will than our own, and so
are without any Unifying Principle to prevent
the conflict of wills which must then arise —
a conflict which must become more and more
destructive the greater the power possessed by
the contending parties, and which, if there were
no counterbalancing power, must result in the
ultimate destruction of the existing race of men.

But there is a counterbalancing power. It is
the very same power used affirmatively instead
of negatively. It is the power of the Personal
with the Impersonal when used under the guidance of that Unifying Principle which the rec-

ognition of the ONE-ness of the Personal
Quality in the Divine Spirit supplies. Those
who are using the creative power of thought
only from the standpoint of individual personality, have obviously less power than those who
are using it from the standpoint of the Personality inherent in the Living Spirit which is the
Source and Fountain of all energy and substance, and therefore in the end the victory
must remain with these latter. And because
the power by which they conquer is that of the
Unifying Personality itself their victory must
result in the establishment of Peace and Happiness throughout the world, and is not a power
of domination but of helpfulness and enlight-
enment. The choice is between these two mot-
toes:—" Each for himself and Devil take the
hindmost," or " God for us all." In proportion, therefore, as we realize the immense
forces dormant in the Impersonal Soul of
Nature, only awaiting the introduction of the
Personal Factor to wake them up into activity
and direct them to specific purposes, the wider
we shall find the scope of the powers within
the reach of man; and the more clearly we perceive the Impersonalness of the very Principle
of Personality itself, the clearer our own proper

position as affording the Differentiating Medium between these two Infinitudes will become to us.

The Impersonalness of the Principle of Personality looks like a contradiction in terms, but it is not. I combine these two seemingly contradictory terms as the best way to convey to the reader the idea of the essential Quality of Personality not yet differentiated into individual centers of consciousness for the doing of particular work. Looked at in this way the Infinite of Personality must have Unity of Purpose for its foundation, for otherwise it would consist of conflicting personalities, in which case we have not yet reached the ONE all-originating cause. Or to put it in another way, an Infinite Personality divided against itself would be an Infinite Insanity, a creator of a cosmic Bedlam which, as a scientific fact, would be impossible of existence. Therefore the conception of an Infinite of Personality necessarily implies a perpetual Unity of Purpose; and for the same reason this Purpose can only be the fuller and fuller expression of an Infinite Unity of Consciousness; and Unity of Consciousness necessarily implies the entire absence of all that would impair it, and therefore its expression can only be as Universal Harmony. If, then, the individual realizes this true nature of the source from which his own consciousness of personality is derived his ideas and work will be based upon this foundation, with the result that as between ourselves peace and good will towards men must accompany this mode of thought, and as between us and the strictly Impersonal Soul of Nature our increasing knowledge in that direction would mean increasing power for carrying out our principle of peace and good will. As this perception of our relation to the Spirit of God and the Soul of Nature spreads from individual to individual so the Kingdom of God will grow, and its universal recognition would be the establishing of the Kingdom of Heaven on earth.

Perhaps the reader will ask why I say the Soul of Nature instead of saying the material universe. The reason is that in using our creative power of Thought we do not operate directly upon material elements — to do that is the work of construction from without and not of creation from within. The whole tendency of modern physical science is to reduce all matter in the final analysis to energy working in a primary ether. Whence this energy and this ether proceed is not the subject of physical analysis. That is a question which cannot be answered by means of the vacuum tube or the spectroscope. Physical science is doing its legitimate work in pushing further and further back the unanalyzable residuum of Nature, but, however far back, an ultimate unanalyzable residuum there must always be; and when physical science brings us to this point it hands us over to the guidance of psychological investigation just as in the Divina Commedia Virgil transfers Dante to the guidance of Beatrice for the study of the higher realms. Various rates of rapidity of motion in this primary ether, producing various numerical combinations of positively and negatively electrified particles, result in the formation of what we know as the different chemical elements, and thus explains the phenomena of their combining quantities, the law by which they join together to form new substances only in certain exact numerical ratios. From the first movement in the primary ether to solid substances, such as wood or iron or our own flesh, is thus a series of vibrations in a succession of mediums, each denser than the preceding one out of which it was concreted and from which it receives the vibratory impulse. This is in effect what physical science has to tell us. But to get further back we must look into the world of the invisible, and it is here that psychological study comes to our aid. We cannot, however, study the invisible side of Nature by working from the outside and so at this point of our studies we find the use of the time-honored teaching regarding the parallelism between the Macrocosm and the Microcosm. If the Microcosm is the reproduction in ourselves of the same principles as exist in the Macrocosm or universe in which we have our being, then by investigating ourselves we shall learn the nature of the corresponding invisible principles in our environment. Here, then, is the application of the dictum of the ancient philosophy, " Know Thyself." It means that the only place where we can study the principles of the invisible side of Nature is in ourselves; and when we know them there we can transfer them to the larger world around us.

In the concluding chapters of my " Edinburgh Lectures on Mental Science " I have outlined the way in which the soul or mind operates upon the physical instrument of its expression, and it resolves itself into this — that the mental action inaugurates a series of vibrations in the etheric body which, in their turn, induce corresponding grosser vibrations in the molecular substance until finally mechanical action is produced on the outside. Now transferring this idea to Nature as a whole we shall see that if our mental action is to affect it in any way it can only be by the response of something at the back of material substance analogous to mind in ourselves; and that there is such a "something" interior to the merely material side of Nature is proved by what we may call the Law of Tendency, not only in animals and plants, but even in inorganic substances, as shown for instance in Professor Bose's work on the Response of Metals. The universal presence of this Law of Tendency therefore indicates the working of some non-material and, so to say, semi-intelligent power in the material world, a power which works perfectly accurately on its own lines so far as it goes, that is to say in a generic manner, but which does not possess that Personal power of *individual selection* which is necessary to bring out the infinite possibilities hidden in it. This is what is meant by the Soul of Nature, and it is for this reason I employ that term instead of saying the material universe. Which term to employ all depends on the mode of action we are contemplating. If it is construction from without, then we are dealing with the purely material universe. If we are seeking to bring about results by the exercise of our mental power from within, then we are dealing with the Soul of Nature. It is that control of the lower degree of intelligence by the higher of which I have spoken in my Edinburgh Lectures.

If we realize what I have endeavored to make clear in the earlier portion of this book, that the whole creation is produced by the operation of the Divine Will upon the Soul of Nature, it will be evident that we can set no limits to the potencies hidden in the latter and capable of being brought out by the operation of the Personal Factor upon it; therefore, granted a sufficiently powerful concentration of will, whether by an individual or a group of individuals, we can well imagine the production of stupendous effects by this agency, and in this way I would explain the statements made in Scripture regarding the marvelous powers to be exercised by the Anti-Christ, whether personal or collective. They are psychic powers, the power of the Soul of Man over the Soul of Nature. But the Soul of Nature is quite impersonal and therefore the moral quality of this action depends entirely on the human operator. This is the point of the Master's teaching regarding the destruction of the fig tree, and it is on this account He adds the warning as to the necessity for clearing our heart of any injurious feeling against others whenever we attempt to make use of this power (Mark xi: 20–26).

According to His teaching, then, this power of controlling the Soul of Nature by the addition of our own Personal Factor, however little we may be able to recognize it as yet, actually exists; its employment depends on our perception of the inner principles common to both, and it is for this reason the ancient wisdom was summed up in the aphorism " Know thyself." No doubt it is a wonderful Knowledge, but on analysis it will be found to be perfectly natural. It is the Knowledge of the cryptic forces of Nature. Now it is remarkable that this ancient maxim inscribed over the portals of the Temple of Delphi is not to be found in the Bible. The Bible maxim is not " Know

thyself" but "Know the Lord." The great
subject of Knowledge is not ourself but "the
Lord"; and herein is the great difference between the two teachings. The one is limited
by human personality, the other is based on
the Infinitude of the Divine Personality; and
because of this it includes human personality
with all its powers over the Soul of Nature. It
is a case of the greater including the less; and
so the whole teaching of Scripture is directed
to bringing us into the recognition of that Divine Personality which is the Great Original in
whose image and likeness we are made. In
proportion as we grow into the recognition of
this our own personality will explain, and the
creative power of our thought will cease to
work invertedly until at last it will work only
on the same principles of Life, Love and Liberty as the Divine Mind, and so all evil will disappear from our world. We shall not, as
some systems teach, be absorbed into Deity
to the extinction of our individual consciousness, but on the contrary our individual consciousness will continually expand, which is
what St. Paul means when he speaks of our
"increasing with the increase of God"—the
continual expanding of the Divine element

within us. But this can only take place by our recognition of ourselves as *receivers* of this Divine element. It is receiving into ourselves of the Divine Personality, a result not to be reached through human reasoning. We reason from premises which we have assumed, and the conclusion is already involved in the premises and can never extend beyond them. But we can only select our premises from among things that we know by experience, whether mental or physical, and accordingly our reasoning is always merely a new placing of the old things. But the receiving of the Divine Personality into ourselves is an entirely New Thing, and so cannot be reached by reasoning from old things. Hence if this Divine ultimate of the Creative Process is to be attained it must be by the Revelation of a New Thing which will afford a new starting-point for our thought, and this New Starting-point is given in the Promise of "the Seed of the Woman" with which the Bible opens. Thenceforward this Promise became the central germinating thought of those who based themselves upon it, thus constituting them a special race, until at last when the necessary conditions had matured the Promised

Seed appeared in Him of whom it is written that He is the express image of God's Person (Heb. I: 3)—that is, the Expression of that Infinite Divine Personality of which I have spoken. "No man hath seen God at any time or can see Him," for the simple reason that Infinitude cannot be the subject of vision. To become visible there must be Individualization, and therefore when Philip said "Show us the Father," Jesus replied, "He that hath seen me hath seen the Father." The Word must become flesh before St. John could say, "That which was from the beginning, which we have heard, which we have seen with our eyes, which we have looked upon, and our hands have handled, of the Word of Life." This is the New Starting-point for the true New Thought — the New Adam of the New Race, each of whom is a new center for the working of the Divine Spirit. This is what Jesus meant when he said, "Except ye eat the flesh and drink the blood of the Son of Man ye have no life in you. My flesh is meat indeed, and my blood is drink indeed —" such a contemplation of the Divine Personality in Him as will cause a like receiving of the Divine Personality into individualization in ourselves

— this is the great purpose of the Creative Process in the individual. It terminates the old series which began with birth after the flesh and inaugurates a New Series by birth after the Spirit, a New Life of infinite unfoldment with glorious possibilities beyond our highest conception.

But all this is logically based upon our recognition of the Personalness of God and of the relation of our individual personality to this Eternal and Infinite Personality, and the result of this is Worship — not an attempt to " butter up " the Almighty and get Him into good temper, but the reverent contemplation of what this Personality must be in Itself; and when we see it to be that Life, Love, Beauty, etc., of which I spoke at the beginning of this book we shall learn to love Him for what He IS, and our prayer will be " Give me more of Thyself." If we realize the great truth that the Kingdom of Heaven is *within* us, that it is the Kingdom of the innermost of our own being and of all creation, and if we realize that this innermost is the place of the Originating Power where Time and Space do not exist and therefore antecedent to all conditions, then we shall see the true meaning of Worship. It is the perception of the Innermost Spirit as eternally subsisting independently of all conditioned manifestation, so that in the true worship our consciousness is removed from the outer sphere of existence to the innermost center of unconditioned being. There we find the Eternal Being of God pure and simple, and we stand reverently in this Supreme Presence knowing that it is the Source of our own being, and wrapt in the contemplation of This, the conditioned is seen to flow out from It. Perceiving this the conditioned passes out of our consideration, for it is seen not to be the Eternal Reality — we have reached that level of consciousness where Time and Space remain no longer. Yet the reverence which the vision of this Supreme Center of all Being cannot fail to inspire is coupled with a sense of feeling quite at home with It. This is because as the Center of *all* Being it is the center of our own being also. It is one-with-ourselves. It is recognizing Itself from our own center of consciousness; so that here we have got back to that Self-contemplation of Spirit which is the first movement of the Creating Power, only now this Self-contemplation is the action of the All-Originating Spirit upon Itself from the center of our own consciousness. So this worship in the Temple of the Innermost is at once reverent adoration and familiar intercourse — not the familiarity that breeds contempt, but a familiarity producing Love, because as it increases we see more clearly the true Life of the Spirit as the continual interaction of Love and Beauty, and the Spirit's recognition of ourselves as an integral portion of Its own Life.

This is not an unpractical dreamy speculation but has a very practical bearing. Death will some day cease to be, for the simple reason that Life alone can be the enduring principle; but we have not yet reached this point in our evolution. Whether any in this generation will reach it I cannot say; but for the rank and file of us the death of the body seems to be by far the more probable event. Now what must this passing out of the body mean to us? It must mean that we find ourselves without the physical vehicle which is the instrument through which our consciousness comes in touch with the external world and all the interests of our present daily life. But the mere putting off of the body does not of itself change the mental attitude; and so if our mind is entirely centered upon these passing interests and external conditions the loss of the instrument by which we held touch with them must involve a consciousness of desire for the only sort of life we have known coupled with a consciousness of our inability to participate in it, which can only result in a consciousness of distress and confusion such as in our present state we cannot imagine.

On the other hand if we have in this world realized the true principle of the Worship of the Eternal Source from which all conditioned life flows out — an inner communing with the Great Reality — we have already passed beyond that consciousness of life which is limited by Time and Space; and so when we put off this mortal body we shall find ourselves upon familiar ground, and therefore not wandering in confusion but quite at home, dwelling in the same light of the Eternal in which we have been accustomed to dwell as an atmosphere enveloping the conditioned life of to-day. Then finding ourselves thus at home on a plane where Time and Space do not exist there will be no question with us of duration. The consciousness will be simply that of peaceful, happy being. That a return to more active personal operation will eventually take place is evidenced by the fact that the basis of all further evolution is the differentiating of the Undifferentiated Life of the Spirit into specific channels of work, through the intermediary of individual personality without which the infinite potentialities of the Creative Law cannot be brought to light.   Therefore, however various our opinions as to its precise form, Resurrection as a principle is a necessity of the creative process.   But such a return to more active life will not mean a return to limitations, but the opening of a new life in which we shall transcend them all, because we have passed beyond the misconception that Time and Space are of the Essence of Life.   When the misconception regarding Time and Space is entirely eradicated all other limitations must disappear because they have their root in this primary one — they are only particular forms of the general proposition.   Therefore though Form with its accompanying relations of Time and Space is necessary for manifestation, these things will be found not to have any force in themselves thus creating limitation, but to be the reflection of the mode of thought which projects them as the expression of itself.

Nor is there any inherent reason why this

process should be delayed till some far-off future. There is no reason why we should not commence at once. No doubt our inherited and personally engendered modes of thought make this difficult, and by the nature of the process it will be only when *all* our thoughts are conformed to this principle that the complete victory will be won. But there must be a commencement to everything, and the more we habituate ourselves to live in that Center of the Innermost where conditions do not exist, the more we shall find ourselves gaining control over outward conditions, because the stream of conditioned life flows out from the Center of Unconditioned Life, and therefore this intrinsic principle of Worship has in it the promise both of the life that now is and of that which is to come. Only we must remember that the really availing worship is that of the Undifferentiated Source *because It is the Source,* and not as a backhanded way of diverting the stream into some petty channel of conditions, for that would only be to get back to the old circle of limitation from which we are seeking to escape.

But if we realize these things we have already laid hold of the Principle of Resurrection, and in point of principle we are already living the resurrection life. What progress we may make in it depends on our practical application of the principle; but simply as principle there is nothing in the principle itself to prevent its complete working at any moment. This is why Jesus did not refer resurrection to some remote point of time but said, " I am the resurrection and the life." No principle can carry in itself an opposite and limiting principle contradictory of its own nature, and this is as true of the Principle of Life as of any other principle. It is we who by our thought introduce an opposite and limiting principle and so hinder the working of the principle we are seeking to bring into operation; but so far as the Principle of Life itself is concerned there is *in it* no reason why it should not come into perfect manifestation here and now.

This, then, is the true purpose of worship. It is to bring us into conscious and loving intercourse with the Supreme Source of our own being, and seeing this we shall not neglect the outward forms of worship. From what we now know they should mean more to us than to others and not less; and in especial if we realize the manifestation of the Divine Personality in

Jesus Christ and its reproduction in Man, we shall not neglect His last command to partake of that sacred memorial to His flesh and blood which He bequeathed to His followers with the words " This do in remembrance of Me."

This holy rite is no superstitious human invention. There are many theories about it, and I do not wish to combat any of them, for in the end they all seem to me to bring us to the same point, that being cleansed from sin by the Divine Love we are now no longer separate from God but become " partakers of the Divine Nature" (II Peter I: 4). This partaking of the Divine Nature could not be more accurately represented than by our partaking of bread and wine as symbols of the Divine Substance and the Divine Life, thus made emblematic of the whole Creative Process from its beginning in the Divine Thought to its completion in the manifestation of that Thought as Perfected Man; and so it brings vividly before us the remembrance of the Personality of God taking form as the Son of Man. We are all familiar with the saying that thoughts become things; and if we affirm the creative power of our own thought as reproducing itself in outward form, how much more must we affirm the same of that Divine Thought which brings the whole universe into existence; so that in accordance with our own principles the Divine Idea of Man was logically bound to show itself in the world of time and space as the Son of God and the Son of man, not two differing natures but one complete whole, thus summing up the foundation principle of all creation in one Undivided Consciousness of Personality. Thus " the Word " or Divine Thought of Man " became flesh," and our partaking of the symbolic elements keeps in our remembrance the supreme truth that this same " Word " or Thought of God in like manner takes form in ourselves as we open our own thought to receive it. And further, if we realize that throughout the universe there is only ONE Originating Life, sending forth only ONE Original Substance as the vehicle for its expression, then it logically follows that *in essence* the bread is a portion of the eternal Substance of God, and the wine a portion of the eternal Life of God. For though the wine is of course also a part of the Universal Substance, we must remember that the Universal Substance is itself a manifestation of the Life of the All-Creating Spirit, and therefore this fluid form of the primary substance has been selected as representing the eternal flowing of the Life of the Spirit into all creation, culminating in its supreme expression in the consciousness of those who, in the recognition of these truths, seek to bring their heart into union with the Divine Spirit. From such considerations as these it will be seen how vast a field of thought is covered by Christ's words " Do this in remembrance of Me."

In conclusion, therefore, do not let yourselves be led astray by any philosophy that denies the Personality of God. In the end it will be found to be a foolish philosophy. No other starting-point of creation is conceivable than the Self-Contemplation of the Divine Spirit, and the logical sequence from this brings us to the ultimate result of the Creative Process in the statement that " if any man be in Christ he is a New creature," or as the margin has it " a new creation " (II Cor. v: 17). Such vain philosophies have only one logical result which is to put *yourself* in the place of God, and then what have you to lean upon in the hour of trial? It is like trying to climb up a ladder that is resting against nothing. Therefore, says the Apostle Paul, " Beware lest any man spoil you through philosophy and vain deceit, after the tradition of man, after the rudiments of the world, and not after Christ." (Col. II: 8.) The teaching of the Bible is sound philosophy, sound reasoning, and sound science because it starts with the sound premises that all Creation proceeds out of God, and that Man is made in the image and likeness of his Creator. It nowhere departs from the Law of Cause and Effect, and by the orderly sequence of this law it brings us at last to the New Creation both in ourselves and in our environment, so that we find the completion of the Creative Process in the declaration " the tabernacle of God is with men " (Rev. xxi: 3), and in the promise " This is the Covenant that I will make with them after those days (i.e., the days of our imperfect apprehension of these things) saith the Lord, I will dwell *in them,* and walk *in them,* and I will be their God, and they shall be my people, and I will put my laws into their hearts, and in their minds will I write them, and their sins and their iniquities will I remember no more " (Heb. x: 16. II Cor. vi: 16. Jeremiah xxxi: 33).

Truly does Bacon say, " A little philosophy

inclineth a man's mind to atheism, but depth in philosophy bringeth men's minds about to religion."— Bacon, Essay, xvi.

THE END

The
DORÉ LECTURES

BY
T. TROWARD

AUTHOR OF
"THE EDINBURGH LECTURES ON MENTAL SCIENCE,"
"BIBLE MYSTERY AND BIBLE MEANING," ETC.

SUNDAY ADDRESSES

AT THE DORÉ GALLERY, LONDON, GIVEN IN CONNEC-
TION WITH THE HIGHER THOUGHT CENTRE,
10, CHENISTON GARDENS, KENSINGTON

Fides et Amor Veritas et Robur

NEW YORK
ROBERT M. McBRIDE & COMPANY
1918

THE TROW PRESS, NEW YORK

CONTENTS.

Kessinger Publishing's Rare Reprints
Thousands of Scarce and Hard-to-Find Books!

- Americana
- Ancient Mysteries
- Animals
- Anthropology
- Architecture
- Arts
- Astrology
- Bibliographies
- Biographies & Memoirs
- Body, Mind & Spirit
- Business & Investing
- Children & Young Adult
- Collectibles
- Comparative Religions
- Crafts & Hobbies
- Earth Sciences
- Education
- Ephemera
- Fiction

- Folklore
- Geography
- Health & Diet
- History
- Hobbies & Leisure
- Humor
- Illustrated Books
- Language & Culture
- Law
- Life Sciences
- Literature
- Medicine & Pharmacy
- Metaphysical
- Music
- Mystery & Crime
- Mythology
- Natural History
- Outdoor & Nature
- Philosophy

- Poetry
- Political Science
- Science
- Psychiatry & Psychology
- Reference
- Religion & Spiritualism
- Rhetoric
- Sacred Books
- Science Fiction
- Science & Technology
- Self-Help
- Social Sciences
- Symbolism
- Theatre & Drama
- Theology
- Travel & Explorations
- War & Military
- Women
- Yoga

We kindly invite you to view our extensive catalog list at:
http://www.kessinger.net

FOREWORD.

THE addresses contained in this volume were delivered by me at the Doré Gallery, Bond Street, London, on the Sundays of the first three months of the present year, and are now published at the kind request of many of my hearers, hence their title of "The Doré Lectures." A number of separate discourses on a variety of subjects necessarily labours under the disadvantage of want of continuity, and also under that of a liability to the frequent repetition of similar ideas and expressions, and the reader will, I trust, pardon these defects as inherent in the circumstances of the work. At the same time it will be found that, although not specially so designed, there is a certain progressive development of thought through the dozen lectures which compose this volume, the reason for which is that they all aim at expressing the same fundamental idea, namely that, though the laws of the universe can never be broken, they can be made to work under special conditions which will produce results that could not be produced under the conditions spontaneously provided by nature. This is a simple scientific principle and it shows us the place which is occupied by the personal factor, that,

v

namely, of an intelligence which sees beyond the present limited manifestation of the Law into its real essence, and which thus constitutes the instrumentality by which the infinite possibilities of the Law can be evoked into forms of power, usefulness, and beauty.

The more perfect, therefore, the working of the personal factor, the greater will be the results developed from the Universal Law; and hence our lines of study should be two-fold—on the one hand the theoretical study of the action of Universal Law, and on the other the practical fitting of ourselves to make use of it; and if the present volume should assist any reader in this two-fold quest, it will have answered its purpose.

The different subjects have necessarily been treated very briefly, and the addresses can only be considered as suggestions for lines of thought which the reader will be able to work out for himself, and he must therefore not expect that careful elaboration of detail which I would gladly have bestowed had I been writing on one of these subjects exclusively. This little book must be taken only for what it is, the record of somewhat fragmentary talks with a very indulgent audience, to whom I gratefully dedicate the volume.

T.T.

June 5, 1909.

ENTERING INTO THE SPIRIT OF IT.

WE all know the meaning of this phrase in our everyday life. The Spirit is that which gives life and movement to anything, in fact it is that which causes it to exist at all. The thought of the author, the impression of the painter, the feeling of the musician, is that without which their works could never have come into being, and so it is only as we enter into the *idea* which gives rise to the work, that we can derive all the enjoyment and benefit from it which it is able to bestow. If we cannot enter into the Spirit of it, the book, the picture, the music, are meaningless to us: to appreciate them we must share the mental attitude of their creator. This is a universal principle; if we do not enter into the Spirit of a thing, it is dead so far as we are concerned; but if we do enter into it we reproduce in ourselves the same quality of life which called that thing into existence.

Now if this is a general principle, why can we not carry it to a higher range of things? Why not to the highest point of all? May we not enter into the originating Spirit of Life itself, and so reproduce it in ourselves as a perennial spring of livingness? This, surely, is a question worthy of our careful consideration.

The spirit of a thing is that which is the source of its inherent movement, and therefore the question before us is, what is the nature of the primal moving power, which is at the back of the endless array of life which we see around us, our own life included? Science gives us ample ground for saying that it is not material, for science has now, at least theoretically, reduced all material things to a primary ether, universally distributed, whose innumerable particles are in absolute equilibrium; whence it follows on mathematical grounds alone that the initial movement which began to concentrate the world and all material substances out of the particles of the dispersed ether, could not have originated in the particles themselves. Thus by a necessary deduction from the conclusions of physical science, we are compelled to realize the presence of some immaterial power capable of separating off certain specific areas for the display of cosmic activity, and then building up a material universe with all its inhabitants by an orderly sequence of evolution, in which each stage lays the foundation for the development of the stage, which is to follow—in a word we find ourselves brought face to face with a power which exhibits on a stupendous scale, the faculties of selection and adaptation of means to ends, and thus distributes energy and life in accordance with a recognizable scheme of cosmic progression. It is therefore not only Life, but also Intelligence, and Life guided by Intelligence becomes Volition. It is this primary originating power which we mean when we speak of " The Spirit," and it is into this Spirit of the whole universe that we must enter if we would reproduce it as a spring of Original Life in ourselves.

Now in the case of the productions of artistic genius we know that we must enter into the movement of the creative mind of the artist, before we can realize the principle which gives rise to his work. We must learn to partake of the feeling, to find expression for which is the motive of his creative activity. May we not apply the same principle to the Greater Creative Mind with which we are seeking to deal? There is something in the work of the artist which is akin to that of original creation. His work, literary, musical, or graphic is original creation on a miniature scale, and in this it differs from that of the engineer, which is constructive, or that of the scientist which is analytical; for the artist in a sense creates something out of nothing, and therefore starts from the stand-point of simple feeling, and not from that of a pre-existing necessity. This, by the hypothesis of the case, is true also of the Parent Mind, for at the stage where the initial movement of creation takes place, there are no existing conditions to compel action in one direction more than another. Consequently the direction taken by the creative impulse is not dictated by outward circumstances, and the primary movement must therefore be entirely due to the action of the Original Mind upon itself; it is the reaching out of this Mind for realization of all that it feels itself to be.

The creative process thus in the first instance is purely a matter of feeling—exactly what we speak of as " motif " in a work of art.

Now it is this original feeling that we need to enter into, because it is the *fons et origo* of the whole chain of causation which subsequently follows. What then can this original feeling of the Spirit be? Since the Spirit is Life-in-itself, its feeling can only be for the fuller expression of Life— any other sort of feeling would be self-destructive and is therefore inconceivable. Then the full expression of Life implies Happiness, and Happiness implies Harmony, and Harmony implies Order, and Order implies Proportion, and Proportion implies Beauty; so that in recognizing the inherent tendency of the Spirit towards the production of Life, we can recognise a similar inherent tendency to the production of these other qualities also; and since the desire to bestow the greater fulness of joyous life can only be described as Love, we can sum up the whole of the feeling which is the original moving impulse in the Spirit as Love and Beauty—the Spirit finding expression through forms of beauty in centres of life, in harmonious reciprocal relation to itself. This is a generalized statement of the broad principle by which Spirit expands from the innermost to the outermost, in accordance with a Law of tendency inherent in itself.

It sees itself, as it were, reflected in various centres of life and energy, each with its appropriate form; but in the first instance these reflections can have no existence except within the originating Mind. They have their first beginning as mental images, so that in addition to the powers of Intelligence and Selection, we must also realise that of Imagination as belonging to the Divine Mind; and we must picture these powers as working from the initial motive of Love and Beauty.

Now this is the Spirit that we need to enter into, and the method of doing so is a perfectly logical one. It is the same method by which all scientific advance is made. It consists in first observing how a certain law works under the conditions spontaneously provided by nature, next in carefully considering what principle this spontaneous working indicates, and lastly deducing from this how the same principle would act under specially selected conditions, not spontaneously provided by nature.

The progress of shipbuilding affords a good example of what I mean. Formerly wood was employed instead of iron, because wood floats in water and iron sinks; yet now the navies of the world are built of iron; careful thought showed the law of floatation to be that anything could float which, bulk for bulk, is lighter than the mass of liquid displaced by it; and so we now make iron float by the very same law by which it sinks, because by the introduction of the *personal* factor, we provide conditions which do not occur spontaneously—according to the esoteric maxim that " Nature unaided fails." Now we want to apply the same process of specializing a generic Law to the first of all Laws, that of the generic life-giving tendency of Spirit itself. Without the element of *individual personality* the Spirit can only work cosmically by a *generic* Law; but this law admits of far higher specialization, and this specialization can only be attained through the introduction of the personal factor. But to introduce this factor the individual must be fully aware of the *principle* which underlies the spontaneous or cosmic action of the law. Where, then, will he find this principle of Life? Certainly not by contemplating Death. In order to get a principle to work in the way we require it to, we must observe its action when it is working spontaneously in this particular direction. We must ask why it goes in the right direction as far as it does—and having learnt this we shall then be able to make it go further. The law of floatation was not discovered by contemplating the sinking of things, but by contemplating the floating of things which floated naturally, and then intelligently asking why they did so.

The knowledge of a principle is to be gained by the study of its affirmative action; when we understand *that* we are in a position to correct the negative conditions which tend to prevent that action.

Now Death is the absence of Life, and disease is the absence of health, so to enter into the Spirit of Life we require to contemplate it, where it is to be found, and not where it is not—we are met with the old question, " Why seek ye the living among the dead? " This is why we start our studies by considering the cosmic creation, for it is there that we find the Life Spirit working through untold ages, not merely as deathless energy, but with a perpetual advance into higher degrees of Life. If we could only so enter into the Spirit as to make it personally *in ourselves* what it evidently is in *itself*, the *magnum opus* would be accomplished. This means realizing our life as drawn direct from the Originating Spirit; and if we now understand that the Thought or Imagination of the Spirit is the great reality of Being, and that all material facts are only correspondences, then it logically follows that what we have to do is to maintain our individual place in the Thought of the Parent Mind.

We have seen that the action of the Originating Mind must needs be *generic*, that is according to types which include multitudes of individuals. This type is the reflection of the Creative Mind at the level of that particular *genius;* and at the human level it is Man, not as associated with particular circumstances, but as existing in the absolute ideal.

In proportion then as we learn to dissociate our conception of ourselves from particular circumstances, and to rest upon our *absolute* nature, as reflections of the Divine ideal, we, in our turn, reflect back into the Divine Imagination its original conception of itself as expressed in generic or typical Man, and so by a natural law of cause and effect, the individual who realizes this mental attitude enters permanently into the Spirit of Life, and it becomes a perennial fountain of Life springing up spontaneously within him.

He then finds himself to be as the Bible says, " the image and likeness of God." He has reached the level at which he affords a new starting point for the creative process, and the Spirit, finding a personal centre in him, begins its work *de novo,* having thus solved the great problem of how to enable the Universal to act directly upon the plane of the Particular.

It is in this sense, as affording the requisite centre for a new departure of the creative Spirit, that man is said to be a " microcosm," or universe in miniature; and this is also what is meant by the esoteric doctrine of the Octave, of which I may be able to speak more fully on some other occasion.

If the principles here stated are carefully considered, they will be found to throw light on much that would otherwise be obscure, and they will also afford the key to the succeeding essays.

The reader is therefore asked to think them out carefully for himself, and to note their connection with the subject of the next article.

INDIVIDUALITY.

INDIVIDUALITY is the necessary complement of the Universal Spirit, which was the subject of our consideration last Sunday. The whole problem of life consists in finding the true relation of the individual to the Universal Originating Spirit; and the first step towards ascertaining this is to realize what the Universal Spirit must be in itself. We have already done this to some extent, and the conclusions we have arrived at are:—

> That the essence of the Spirit is Life, Love, and Beauty.
>
> That its Motive, or primary moving impulse, is to express the Life, Love and Beauty which it feels itself to be.
>
> That the Universal cannot act on the plane of the Particular except by becoming the particular, that is by expression through the individual.

If these three axioms are clearly grasped, we have got a solid foundation from which to start our consideration of the subject for to-day.

The first question that naturally presents itself is,

10

If these things be so, why does not every individual express the life, love, and beauty of the Universal Spirit? The answer to this question is to be found in the Law of Consciousness. We cannot be conscious of anything except by realizing a certain relation between it and ourselves. It must affect us in some way, otherwise we are not conscious of its existence; and according to the way in which it affects us we recognize ourselves as standing related to it. It is this self-recognition on our own part carried out to the sum total of all our relations, whether spiritual, intellectual, or physical, that constitutes our realization of life. On this principle, then, for the *realization* of its own Livingness, the production of centres of life, through its relation to which this conscious realization can be attained, becomes a necessity for the Originating Mind. Then it follows that this realization can only be complete where the individual has perfect liberty to withhold it; for otherwise no true realization could have taken place. For instance, let us consider the working of Love. Love must be spontaneous, or it has no existence at all. We cannot imagine such a thing as mechanically induced love. But anything which is formed so as to automatically produce an effect without any volition of its own, is nothing but a piece of mechanism. Hence if the Originating Mind is to realize the reality of Love, it can only be by relation to some being which has the power to withhold love. The same applies to the realization of all the other modes of livingness; so that it is only in proportion, as the individual life is an independent centre of action, with the option of acting either positively or negatively, that any real life has been produced at all. The further the created thing is from being a merely mechanical arrangement, the higher is the grade of creation. The solar system is a perfect work of mechanical creation, but to constitute centres which can reciprocate the highest nature of the Divine Mind, requires not a mechanism, however perfect, but a mental centre which is, in itself, an independent source of action. Hence by the requirements of the case man should be capable of placing himself either in a positive or a negative relation to the Parent Mind, from which he originates; otherwise he would be nothing more than a clockwork figure.

In this necessity of the case, then, we find the reason why the life, love, and beauty of the Spirit are not visibly reproduced in every human being. They *are* reproduced in the world of nature, so far as a mechanical and automatic action can represent them, but their perfect reproduction can only take place on the basis of a liberty akin to that of the Originating Spirit itself, which therefore implies the liberty of negation as well as of affirmation.

Why, then, does the individual make a negative choice? Because he does not understand the law of his own individuality, and believes it to be a law of limitation, instead of a Law of Liberty. He does not expect to find the starting point of the Creative Process reproduced within himself, and so he looks to the mechanical side of things for the basis of his reasoning about life. Consequently his reasoning lands him in the conclusion that life is limited, because he has assumed limitation in his premises, and so logically cannot escape from it in his conclusion. Then he thinks that this is the law and so ridicules the idea of transcending it. He points to the sequence of cause and effect, by which death, disease, and disaster, hold their sway over the individual, and says that sequence is law. And he is perfectly right so far as he goes—it is *a* law; but not *the* Law. When we have only reached this stage of comprehension, we have yet to learn that a higher law can include a lower one so completely as entirely to swallow it up.

The fallacy involved in this negative argument, is the assumption that the law of limitation is essential in all grades of being. It is the fallacy of the old shipbuilders as to the impossibility of building iron ships. What is required is to get at the *principle* which is at the back of the Law in its affirmative working, and specialize it under higher conditions than are spontaneously presented by nature, and this can only be done by the introduction of the personal element, that is to say an individual intelligence capable of comprehending the principle. The question, then, is, what is the principle by which we came into being? and this is only a personal application of the general question, How did anything come into being? Now, as I pointed out in the preceding article, the ultimate deduction from physical science is that the originating movement takes place in the Universal Mind, and is analogous to that of our own imagination; and as we have just seen, the perfect ideal can only be that of a being capable of reciprocating *all* the qualities of the Originating Mind. Consequently man, in his inmost nature, is the product of the Divine Mind imaging forth an image of itself on the plane of the relative as the complementary to its own sphere of the absolute.

If we will therefore go to the *inmost* principle in ourselves, which philosophy and Scripture alike declare to be made in the image and likeness of God, instead of to the outer vehicles which it externalizes as instruments through which to function on the various planes of being, we shall find that we have reached a principle in ourselves which stands in *loco dei* towards all our vehicles and also towards our environment. It is above them all, and creates them, however unaware we may be of the fact, and relatively to them it occupies the place of first cause. The recognition of this is the discovery of our own relation to the whole world of the relative. On the other hand this must not lead us into the mistake of supposing that there is nothing higher, for, as we have already seen, this inmost principle or *ego* is itself the effect of an antecedent cause, for it proceeds from the imaging process in the Divine Mind.

We thus find ourselves holding an intermediate position between true First Cause, on the one hand, and the world of secondary causes on the other, and in order to understand the nature of this position, we must fall back on the axiom that the Universal can only work on the plane of the Particular through the individual. Then we see that the function of the individual is to *differentiate* the undistributed flow of the Universal into suitable directions for starting different trains of secondary causation.

Man's place in the cosmic order is that of a distributor of the Divine power, subject, however, to the inherent Law of the power which he distributes. We see one instance of this in ordinary science, in the fact that we never create force; all we can do is to distribute it. The very word Man means distributor or measurer, as in common with all words derived from the Sanderit root MN., it implies the idea of measurement, just as in the words moon, month, mens, mind, and " man," the Indian weight of 8olbs.; and it is for this reason that man is spoken of in Scripture as a " steward," or dispenser of the Divine gifts. As our minds become open to the full meaning of this position, the immense possibilities and also the responsibility contained in it will become apparent.

It means that the individual is the creative centre of his own world. Our past experience affords no evidence against this, but on the contrary, is evidence for it. Our true nature is always present, only we have hitherto taken the lower and mechanical side of things for our starting point, and so have created limitation instead of expansion. And even with the knowledge of the Creative Law which we have now attained, we shall continue to do this, if we seek our starting point in the things which are below us and not in the only thing which is above us, namely the Divine Mind, because it is only there that we can find illimitable Creative Power. Life is *being*, it is the experience of states of consciousness, and there is an unfailing correspondence between these inner states and our outward conditions. Now we see from the Original Creation that the state of consciousness must be the cause, and the corresponding conditions the effect, because at the starting of the creation no conditions existed, and the working of the Creative Mind upon itself can only have been a state of consciousness. This, then, is clearly the Creative Order—from states to conditions. But we invert this order, and seek to create from conditions to states. We say, If I had such and such conditions they would produce the state of feeling which I desire; and in so saying we run the risk of making a mistake as to the correspondence, for it may turn out that the particular conditions which we fixed on are not such as would produce the desired state. Or, again, though they might produce it in a certain degree, other conditions might produce it in a still greater degree, while at the same time opening the way to the attainment of still higher states and still better conditions. Therefore our wisest plan is to follow the pattern of the Parent Mind and make mental self-recognition our starting point, knowing that by the inherent Law of Spirit the corelated conditions will come by a natural process of growth. Then the great self-recognition is that of our relation to the Supreme Mind. That is the generating centre and we are distributing centres; just as electricity is generated at the central station and delivered in different forms of power by reason of passing through appropriate centres of distribution, so that in one place it lights a room, in another conveys a message, and in a third drives a

tram car.   In like manner the power of the Universal Mind takes particular forms through the particular mind of the individual.   It does not interfere with the lines of his individuality, but works
along them, thus making him, not less, but more
himself.   It is thus, not a compelling power, but
an expanding and illuminating one; so that the more
the individual recognizes the reciprocal action between it and himself, the more full of life he must
become.

Then also we need not be troubled about future
conditions because we know that the All-originating
Power is working through us and for us, and that
according to the Law proved by the whole existing
creation, it produces all the conditions required for
the expression of the Life, Love and Beauty which
it is, so that we can fully trust it to open the way as
we go along.   The Great Teacher's words, " Take
no thought for the morrow "—and note that the
correct translation is " Take no anxious thought "—
are the practical application of the soundest philosophy.   This does not, of course, mean that we
are not to exert ourselves.   We must do our share
in the work, and not expect God to do *for* us what
He can only do *through* us.   We are to use our
common sense and natural faculties in working
upon the conditions now present.   We must make
use of them, *as far as they go,* but we must not try

and go further than the present things require; we must not try to force things, but allow them to grow naturally, knowing that they are doing so under the guidance of the All-Creating Wisdom.

Following this method we shall grow more and more into the habit of looking to mental attitude as the Key to our progress in Life, knowing that everything else must come out of that; and we shall further discover that our mental attitude is eventually determined by the way in which we regard the Divine Mind. Then the final result will be that we shall see the Divine Mind to be nothing else than Life, Love and Beauty—Beauty being identical with Wisdom or the perfect adjustment of parts to whole—and we shall see ourselves to be distributing centres of these primary energies and so in our turn subordinate centres of creative power. And as we advance in this knowledge we shall find that we transcend one law of limitation after another by finding the higher law, of which the lower is but a partial expression, until we shall see clearly before us, as our ultimate goal, nothing less than the Perfect Law of Liberty—not liberty without Law which is anarchy, but Liberty according to Law. In this way we shall find that the Apostle spoke the literal truth, when he said, that we shall become like Him when we see Him *as He is*, because the whole process by which our individuality is produced is one of reflection of the image existing in the Divine Mind. When we thus learn the Law of our own being we shall be able to specialize it in ways of which we have hitherto but little conception, but as in the case of all natural laws the specialization cannot take place until the fundamental principle of the generic law has been fully realized. For these reasons the student should endeavour to realize more and more perfectly, both in theory and practice, the law of the relation between the Universal and the Individual Minds. It is that of *reciprocal* action. If this fact of reciprocity is grasped, it will be found to explain both why the individual falls short of expressing the fulness of Life, which the Spirit is, and why he can attain to the fulness of that expression; just as the same law explains why iron sinks in water, and how it can be made to float. It is the individualizing of the Universal Spirit, by recognizing its reciprocity to ourselves, that is the secret of the perpetuation and growth of our own individuality.

THE NEW THOUGHT AND THE NEW ORDER.

In the two preceding lectures I have endeavoured to reach some conception of what the All-originating Spirit is in itself, and of the relation of the individual to it. So far as we can form any conception of these things at all we see that they are universal principles applicable to all nature, and, at the human level, applicable to all men: they are general laws the recognition of which is an essential preliminary to any further advance, because progress is made, not by setting aside the inherent law of things, which is impossible, but by specializing it through presenting conditions which will enable the same principle to act in a less limited manner. Having therefore got a general idea of these two ultimates, the universal and the individual, and of their relation to one another, let us now consider the process of specialization. In what does the specialization of a natural law consist? It consists in making that law or principle produce an effect which it could not produce under the simply generic conditions spontaneously provided by nature.

This selection of suitable conditions is the work of Intelligence, it is a process of consciously arranging things in a new order, so as to produce a new result. The principle is never new, for principles are eternal and universal; but the knowledge that the same principle will produce new results when working under new conditions is the key to the unfoldment of infinite possibilities. What we have therefore to consider is the working of Intelligence in providing specific conditions for the operation of universal principles, so as to bring about new results which will transcend our past experiences. The process does not consist in the introduction of new elements, but in making new combinations of elements which are always present; just as our ancestors had no conception of carriages that could go without horses, and yet by a suitable combination of elements which were always in existence, such vehicles are common objects in our streets to-day. How, then, is the power of Intelligence to be brought to bear upon the generic law of the relation between the Individual and the Universal so as to specialize it into the production of greater results than those which we have hitherto obtained?

All the practical attainments of science, which place the civilized world of to-day in advance of the times of King Alfred or Charlemagne, have been gained by a uniform method, and that a very simple one. It is by always enquiring what is the affirmative factor in any existing combination, and asking ourselves why, in that particular combination, it does not act beyond certain limits. What makes the thing a success, so far as it goes, and what prevents it going further? Then, by carefully considering the nature of the affirmative factor, we see what sort of conditions to provide to enable it to express itself more fully. This is the scientific method; it has proved itself true in respect of material things, and there is no reason why it should not be equally reliable in respect of spiritual things also.

Taking this as our method, we ask, What is the affirmative factor in the whole creation, and in ourselves as included in the creation, and, as we found in the first lecture, this factor is Spirit—that invisible power which concentrates the primordial ether into forms, and endows those forms with various modes of motion, from the simply mechanical motion of the planet up to the volitional motion in man. And, since this is so, the primary affirmative factor can only be the Feeling and the Thought of the Universal Spirit.* Now, by the hypothesis of the case, the Universal Spirit must be the Pure Essence of Life, and therefore its feeling and

* See my " Edinburgh Lectures on Mental Science."

thought can only be towards the continually increasing expression of the livingness which it is; and accordingly the specialization, of which we are in search, must be along the line of affording it a centre from which it may more perfectly realize this feeling and express this thought: in other words the way to specialize the generic principle of Spirit is by providing new mental conditions in consonance with its own original nature.

The scientific method of enquiry therefore brings us to the conclusion that the required conditions for translating the racial or generic operation of the Spirit into a specialized individual operation is a new way of *thinking*—a mode of thought concurring with, and not in opposition to, the essential forward movement of the Creative Spirit itself. This implies an entire reversal of our old conceptions. Hitherto we have taken forms and conditions as the starting point of our thought and inferred that *they* are the causes of mental states; now we have learnt that the true order of the creative process is exactly the reverse, and that thought and feeling are the causes, and forms and conditions the effects. When we have learnt this lesson we have grasped the foundation principle on which individual specialization of the generic law of the creative process becomes a practical possibility.

New Thought, then, is not the name of a particular sect, but is the essential factor by which our own future development is to be carried on; and its essence consists in seeing the relation of things in a New Order. Hitherto we have inverted the true order of cause and effect; now, by carefully considering the real nature of the Principle of Causation in itself—*causa causans* as distinguished from *causa causata*—we return to the true order and adopt a new method of thinking in accordance with it.

In themselves this order and this method of thinking are not new. They are older than the foundation of the world, for they are those of the Creative Spirit itself; and all through the ages this teaching has been handed down under various forms, the true meaning of which has been perceived only by a few in each generation. But as the light breaks in upon any individual it is a new light to him, and so to each one in succession it becomes the New Thought. And when anyone reaches it, he finds himself in a New Order. He continues indeed to be included in the universal order of the cosmos, but in a perfectly different way to what he had previously supposed; for, from his new standpoint, he finds that he is included, not so much as a part of the general effect, but as a part of the general cause; and when he perceives this he then sees that the method of his further advance must be by letting the General Cause flow more and more freely into his own specific centre, and he therefore seeks to provide thought conditions which will enable him to do so.

Then, still employing the scientific method of following up the affirmative factor, he realizes that this universal causative power, by whatever name he may call it, manifests as Supreme Intelligence in the adaptation of means to ends. It does so in the mechanism of the planet, in the production of supply for the support of physical life, and in the maintenance of the race as a whole. True, the investigator is met at every turn with individual failure; but his answer to this is that there is no cosmic failure, and that the apparent individual failure is itself a part of the cosmic process, and will diminish in proportion as the individual attains to the recognition of the Moving Principle of that process, and provides the necessary conditions to enable it to take a new starting point in his own individuality. Now, one of these conditions is to recognize it as Intelligence, and to remember that when working through our own mentality it in no way changes its essential nature, just as electricity loses none of its essential qualities in passing through the special apparatus which enables it to manifest as light.

When we see this, our line of thought will run something as follows:—" My mind is a centre of

Divine operation. The Divine operation is always for expansion and fuller expression, and this means the production of something beyond what has gone before, something entirely new, not included in past experience, though proceeding out of it by an orderly sequence of growth. Therefore, since the Divine cannot change its inherent nature, it must operate in the same manner in me; consequently in my own special world, of which I am the centre, it will move forward to produce new conditions, always in advance of any that have gone before." This is a legitimate line of argument, from the premises established in the recognition of the relation between the individual and the Universal Mind; and it results in our looking to the Divine Mind, not only as creative, but also as directive— that is as determining the actual forms which the conditions for its manifestation will take in our own particular world, as well as supplying the energy for their production. We miss the point of the relation between the individual and the universal, if we do not see that the Originating Spirit is a *forming* power. It is the forming power throughout nature, and if we would specialize it we must learn to trust its formative quality when operating from its new starting point in ourselves.

But the question naturally arises, If this is so, what part is taken by the individual? Our part is

to provide a concrete centre round which the Divine
energies can play. In the generic order of being
we exercise upon it a force of attraction in accordance with the innate pattern of our particular individuality; and as we begin to realize the Law of this
relation, we, in our turn, are attracted towards the
Divine along the lines of least resistance, that is on
those lines which are most natural to our special
bent of mind. In this way we throw out certain
aspirations with the result that we intensify our
attraction of the Divine forces in a certain specific
manner, and they then begin to act both through us
and around us in accordance with our aspirations.
This is the rationale of the reciprocal action between the Universal Mind and the individual mind,
and this shows us that our desires should not be
directed so much to the acquisition of particular
things as to the reproduction in ourselves of particular phases of the Spirit's activity; and this, being
in its very nature creative, is bound to externalize
as corresponding things and circumstances. Then,
when these external facts appear in the circle of our
objective life, we must work upon them from the
objective stand-point. This is where many fall short
of completed work. They realize the subjective or
creative process, but do not see that it must be
followed by an objective or constructive process,
and consequently they are unpractical dreamers and

never reach the stage of completed work. The creative process brings the materials and conditions for the work to our hands; then we must make use of them with diligence and common-sense—God will provide the food, but He will not cook the dinner.

This, then, is the part taken by the individual, and it is thus that he becomes a distributing centre of the Divine energy, neither on the one hand trying to lead it like a blind force, nor on the other being himself under a blind unreasoning impulse from it. He receives guidance because he seeks guidance; and he both seeks and receives according to a Law which he is able to recognize; so that he no more sacrifices his liberty or dwarfs his powers, than does an engineer who submits to the generic laws of electricity, in order to apply them to some specific purpose. The more intimate his knowledge of this Law of Reciprocity becomes, the more he finds that it leads on to Liberty, on the same principle by which we find in physical science that nature obeys us precisely in the same degree to which we first obey nature. As the esoteric maxim has it " What is a truth on one plane is a truth on all." But the key to this enfranchisement of body, mind, and circumstances is in that new thought which becomes creative of new conditions, because it realizes the true order of the creative process.

Therefore it is that, if we would bring a new order of Life, Light, and Liberty into our lives we must commence by bringing a new order into our thought, and find in ourselves the starting point of a new creative series, not by the force of personal will, but by union with the Divine Spirit, which in the expression of its inherent Love and Beauty, makes all things new.

THE LIFE OF THE SPIRIT.

THE three preceding lectures have touched upon certain fundamental truths in a definite order—first the nature of the Originating Spirit itself, next the generic relation of the individual to this All-embracing Spirit, and lastly the way to specialize this relation so as to obtain greater results from it than spontaneously arise by its merely generic action, and we have found that this can only be done through a new order of thought. This sequence is logical because it implies a Power, an Individual who understands the Power, and a Method of applying the power deduced from understanding its nature. These are general principles without realizing which it is impossible to proceed further, but assuming that the reader has grasped their significance, we may now go on to consider their application in greater detail.

Now this application must be a personal one, for it is only through the individual that the higher specialization of the power can take place, but at the same time this must not lead us to suppose that the individual, himself, brings the creative force into being. To suppose this is inversion; and we cannot impress upon ourselves too deeply that the relation of the individual to the Divine Spirit is that of a distributor, and not that of the original creator. If this is steadily borne in mind the way will become clear, otherwise we shall be led into confusion.

What, then, is the Power which we are to distribute? It is the Originating Spirit itself. We are sure that it is this because the new order of thought always begins at the beginning of any series which it contemplates bringing into manifestation, and it is based upon the fact that the origin of everything is Spirit. It is in this that its creative power resides; hence the person who is in the true new order of thought assumes as an axiomatic fact that what he has to distribute, or differentiate into manifestation is nothing else than the Originating Spirit. This being the case, it is evident that the *purpose* of the distribution must be the more perfect expression of the Originating Spirit as that which it is in itself, and what it is in itself is emphatically Life. What is seeking for expression, then, is the perfect Livingness of the Spirit; and this expression is to be found, through ourselves, by means of our renewed mode of thought. Let us see, then, how our new order of thought, with regard to the Principle of Life, is likely to operate.

In our old order of thought we have always associated Life with the physical body—life has been for us the supreme physical fact. Now, however, we know that Life is much more than this; but, as the greater includes the less, it includes physical life as one mode of its manifestation. The true order does not require us to deny the reality of physical life or to call it an illusion; on the contrary it sees in physical life the completion of a great creative series, but it assigns it the proper place in that series, which is what the old mode of thought did not.

When we realize the truth about the Creative Process, we see that the originating life is not physical: its livingness consists in thought and feeling. By this inner movement it throws out vehicles through which to function, and these become living forms because of the inner principle which is sustaining them; so that the Life with which we are primarily concerned in the new order is the life of thought and feeling in ourselves as the vehicle, or distributing medium, of the Life of the Spirit.

Then, if we have grasped the idea of the Spirit as the great *forming* Power, as stated in the last lecture, we shall seek in it the fountain-head of Form as well as of Power: and as a logical deduction from this we shall look to it to give form to our thoughts and feelings. If the principle is once recognised the sequence is obvious. The form taken by our outward conditions, whether of body or circumstance, depends on the form taken by our thoughts and feelings, and our thoughts and feelings will take form from that source from which we allow them to receive suggestion. Accordingly if we allow them to accept their fundamental suggestions from the relative and limited, they will assume a corresponding form and transmit them to our external environment, thus repeating the old order of limitation in a ceaselessly recurring round. Now our object is to get out of this circle of limitation, and the only way to do so is to get our thoughts and feelings moulded into new forms continually advancing to greater and greater perfection. To meet this requirement, therefore, there must be a forming power greater than that of our own unaided conceptions, and this is to be found in our realization of the Spirit as the Supreme Beauty, or Wisdom, moulding our thoughts and feelings into shapes harmoniously adjusted to the fullest expression, in and through us, of the Livingness which Spirit is in itself.

Now this is nothing more than transferring to the innermost plane of origination, a principle with which all readers who are " in the thought " may be presumed to be quite familiar—the principle of

Receptiveness. We all know what is meant by a receptive mental attitude when applied to healing or telepathy; and does it not logically follow that the same principle may be applied to the receiving of life itself from the Supreme Source? What is wanted, therefore, is to place ourselves in a receptive mental attitude towards the Universal Spirit with the intention of receiving its forming influence into our mental substance. It is always the presence of a definite intention that distinguishes the intelligent receptive attitude of mind from a merely sponge-like absorbancy, which sucks in any and every influence that may happen to be floating round: for we must not shut our eyes to the fact that there are various influences in the mental atmosphere by which we are surrounded, and some of them of the most undesirable kind. Clear and definite intention is therefore as necessary in our receptive attitude as in our active and creative one; and if our intention is to have our own thoughts and feelings moulded into such forms as to express those of the Spirit, then we establish that relation to the Spirit which, by the conditions of the case, must necessarily lead us to the conception of new ideals vitalised by a power which will enable us to bring them into concrete manifestation. It is in this way that we become differentiating centres of the Divine Thought giving it expression in form in the world of space and time, and thus is solved the great problem of enabling the Universal to act upon the plane of the particular without being hampered by those limitations which the merely generic law of manifestation imposes upon it. It is just here that subconscious mind performs the function of a " bridge " between the finite and the infinite as noted in my " Edinburgh Lectures on Mental Science " (page 31), and it is for this reason that a recognition of its susceptibility to impression is so important.

By establishing, then, a personal relation to the life of the Spirit, the sphere of the individual becomes enlarged. The reason is that he allows a greater intelligence than his own to take the initiative; and since he knows that this Intelligence is also the very Principle of Life itself, he cannot have any fear that it will act in any way to the diminution of his individual life, for that would be to stultify its own operation—it would be self-destructive action which is a contradiction in terms to the conception of Creative Spirit. Knowing, then, that by its inherent nature this Intelligence can only work to the expansion of the individual life, we can rest upon it with the utmost confidence and trust it to take an initiative which will lead to far greater results than any we could forecast from the stand-point of our own knowledge. So long as we insist on dictating the particular form which the action of the Spirit is to take, we limit it, and so close against ourselves avenues of expansion which might otherwise have been open to us; and if we ask ourselves why we do this we shall find that in the last resort it is because we do not believe in the Spirit as a *forming* power. We have, indeed, advanced to the conception of it as executive power, which will work to a prescribed pattern, but we have yet to grasp the conception of it as versed in the art of design, and capable of elaborating schemes of construction, which will not only be complete in themselves, but also in perfect harmony with one another. When we advance to the conception of the Spirit as containing in itself the ideal of Form as well as of Power, we shall cease from the effort of trying to force things into a particular shape, whether on the inner or the outer plane, and shall be content to trust the inherent harmoniousness or Beauty of the Spirit to produce combinations far in advance of anything that we could have conceived ourselves. This does not mean that we shall reduce ourselves to a condition of apathy, in which all desire, expectation and enthusiasm have been quenched, for these are the mainspring of our mental machinery; but on the contrary their action will be quickened by the knowledge that there is working at the back of

them a Formative Principle so infallible that it cannot miss its mark; so that however good and beautiful the existing forms may be, we may always rest
in the happy expectation of something still better
to come. And it will come by a natural law of
growth, because the Spirit is in itself the Principle
of Increase. They will grow out of present conditions for the simple reason that if you are to reach
some further point it can only be by starting from
where you are now. Therefore it is written, " Des-
pise not the day of small things." There is only
one proviso attached to this forward movement of
the Spirit in the world of our own surroundings,
and that is that we shall co-operate with it; and
this co-operation consists in making the best use
of existing conditions in cheerful reliance on the
Spirit of Increase to express itself through us, and
for us, because we are in harmony with it. This
mental attitude will be found of immense value
in setting us free from worry and anxiety,
and as a consequence our work will be done
in a much more efficient manner. We shall
do the present work *for its own sake,* knowing
that herein is the principle of unfoldment; and doing it simply for its own sake we shall bring to
bear upon it a power of concentration which cannot fail of good results—and this quite naturally
and without any toilsome effort. We shall then

find that the secret of co-operation is to have faith in ourselves because we first have faith in God; and we shall discover that this Divine self-confidence is something very different from a boastful egotism which assumes a personal superiority over others. It is simply the assurance of a man who knows that he is working in accordance with a law of nature. He does not claim as a personal achievement what the Law does *for* him: but on the other hand he does not trouble himself about outcries against his presumptuous audacity raised by persons who are ignorant of the Law which he is employing. He is therefore neither boastful nor timorous, but simply works on in cheerful expectancy because he knows that his reliance is upon a Law which cannot be broken.

In this way, then, we must realize the Life of the Spirit as being also the Law of the Spirit. The two are identical, and cannot deny themselves. Our recognition of them gives them a new starting point through our own mentality, but they still continue to be the same in their nature, and unless limited or inverted by our mental affirmation of limited or inverted conditions, they are bound to work out into fuller and continually fuller expression of the Life, Love, and Beauty which the Spirit is in itself. Our path, therefore, is plain; it is simply to contemplate the Life, Love, and Beauty of the Originating Spirit and affirm that we are already giving expression to it in our thoughts and in our actions however insignificant they may at present appear. This path may be very narrow and humble in its beginning, but it ever grows wider and mounts higher, for it is the continually expanding expression of the Life of the Spirit which is infinite and knows no limits.

ALPHA AND OMEGA.

ALPHA and Omega, the First and the Last. What does this mean? It means the entire series of causation from the first originating movement to the final and completed result. We may take this on any scale from the creation of a cosmos to the creation of a lady's robe. Everything has its origin in an idea, a thought; and it has its completion in the manifestation of that thought in form. Many intermediate stages are necessary, but the Alpha and Omega of the series are the thought and the thing. This shows us that in essence the thing already existed in the thought. Omega is already potential in Alpha, just as in the Pythagorean system all numbers are said to proceed from unity and to be resolvable back again into it. Now it is this general principle of the already existence of the thing in the thought that we have to lay hold of, and as we find it true in an architect's design of the house that is to be, so we find it true in the great work of the Architect of the Universe. When we see this we have realized a general principle, which we find at work everywhere. That is

41

the meaning of a *general* principle: it can be applied to any sort of subject; and the use of studying general principles is to give them particular application to anything we may have to deal with. Now what we have to deal with most of all is ourselves, and so we come to the consideration of Alpha and Omega in the human being. In the vision of St. John, the speaker of the words, "I am Alpha and Omega, the First and the Last," is described as "Like unto a son of man"—that is, however transcendent the appearance in the vision, it is essentially human, and thus suggests to us the presence of the universal principle at the human level. But the figure in the apocalyptic vision is not that of man as we ordinarily know him. It is that of Omega as it subsists enshrined in Alpha: it is the ideal of humanity as it subsists in the Divine Mind which was manifested in objective form to the eyes of the seer, and therefore presented the Alpha and Omega of that idea in all the majesty of Divine glory.

But if we grasp the truth that the thing is already existent in the thought, do we not see that this transcendent Omega must be already existent in the Divine ideal of every one of us? If on the plane of the absolute time is not, then does it not follow that this glorified humanity is a present fact in the Divine Mind? And if this is so, then this fact is eternally true regarding every human being. But if it is true that the thing exists in the thought, it is equally true that the thought finds form in the thing; and since things exist under the relative conditions of time and space, they are necessarily subject to a law of Growth, so that while the subsistence of the thing in the thought is perfect *ab initio*, the expression of the thought in the thing is a matter of gradual development. This is a point which we must never lose sight of in our studies; and we must never lose sight of the perfection of the thing in the thought because we do not yet see the perfection of the thought in the thing. Therefore we must remember that man, as we know him now, has by no means reached the ultimate of his evolution. We are only yet in the making, but we have now reached a point where we can facilitate the evolutionary process by conscious co-operation with the Creative Spirit. Our share in this work commences with the recognition of the Divine ideal of man, and thus finding the pattern by which we are to be guided. For since the person to be created after this pattern is ourself, it follows that, by whatever processes the Divine ideal transforms itself into concrete reality, the place where those processes are to work must be within ourselves; in other words, the creative action of the Spirit takes place through the laws of our own mentality. If it is a true maxim that the thing must take form in the thought before the thought can take form in the thing, then it is plain that the Divine Ideal can only be externalized in our objective life in proportion as it is first formed in our thought; and it takes form in our thought only to the extent to which we apprehend its existence in the Divine Mind. By the nature of the relation between the individual mind and the Universal Mind it is strictly a case of reflection; and in proportion as the mirror of our own mind blurs or clearly reflects the image of the Divine ideal, so will it give rise to a correspondingly feeble or vigorous reproduction of it in our external life.

This being the rationale of the matter, why should we limit our conception of the Divine ideal of ourselves? Why should we say, " I am too mean a creature ever to reflect so glorious an image "— or " God never intended such a limitless ideal to be reproduced in human beings." In saying such things we expose our ignorance of the whole Law of the Creative Process. We shut our eyes to the fact that the Omega of completion already subsists in the Alpha of conception, and that the Alpha of conception would be nothing but a lying illusion if it was not capable of expression in the Omega of completion. The creative process in us is that we become the individual reflection of what we realize

God to be relatively to ourselves, and therefore if we realize the Divine Spirit as the *infinite potential* of all that can constitute a perfected human being, this conception must, by the Law of the Creative Process, gradually build up a corresponding image in our mind, which in turn will act upon our external conditions.

This, by the laws of mind, is the nature of the process and it shows us what St. Paul means when he speaks of Christ being formed in us (Gal. iv. 19) and what in another place he calls being renewed in knowledge after the image of Him that created us (Col. iii. 10). It is a thoroughly logical sequence of cause and effect, and what we require is to see more clearly the Law of this sequence and use it intelligently—that is why St. Paul says it is being " renewed in knowledge ": it is a New Knowledge, the recognition of principles which we had not previously apprehended. Now the fact which, in our past experience, we have not grasped is that the human mind forms a new point of departure for the work of the Creative Spirit; and in proportion as we see this more and more clearly, the more we shall find ourselves entering into a new order of life in which we become less and less subject to the old limitations. This is not a reward arbitrarily bestowed upon us for holding dogmatically to certain mere verbal statements, but it is the natural result

of understanding the supreme law of our own being. On its own plane it is as purely scientific as
the law of chemical re-action; only here we are not
dealing with the interaction of secondary causes
but with the Self-originating action of Spirit. Hence
a new force has to be taken into account which
does not occur in physical science, the power of
Feeling. Thought creates form, but it is feeling
that gives vitality to thought. Thought without
feeling may be constructive as in some great engi-
neering work, but it can never be creative as in the
work of the artist or musician; and that which originates within itself a new order of causation is, so
far as all pre-existing forms are concerned, a creation *ex nihilo,* and is therefore Thought expressive
of Feeling. It is this indissoluble union of
Thought and Feeling that distinguishes creative
thought from merely analytical thought and places
it in a different category; and therefore if we are to
afford a new starting-point for carrying on the work
of creation it must be by assimilating the feeling
of the Originating Spirit as part and parcel of its
thought—it is that entering into the Mind of the
Spirit of which I spoke in the first address.

Now the images in the Mind of the Spirit must
necessarily be *generic.* The reason for this is that
by its very nature the Principle of Life must be
prolific, that is, tending to Multiplicity, and there-

fore the original Thought-image must be fundamental to whole races, and not exclusive to particular individuals. Consequently the images in the Mind of the Spirit must be absolute types of the true essentials of the perfect development of the race, just what Plato meant by architypal ideas. This is the perfect subsistence of the thing in the thought. Therefore it is that our evolution as centres of *creative* activity, the exponents of new laws, and through them of new conditions, depends on our realizing in the Divine Mind the architype of mental perfection, at once as thought and feeling. But when we find all this in the Divine Mind, do we not meet with an infinite and glorious Personality? There is nothing lacking of all that we can understand by Personality, excepting outward form; and since the very essence of telepathy is that it dispenses with the physical presence, we find ourselves in a position of interior communion with a Personality at once Divine and Human. This is that Personality of the Spirit which St. John saw in the apocalyptic vision, and which by the very conditions of the case is the Alpha and Omega of Humanity.

But, as I have said, it is simply *generic* in itself, and it becomes active and specific only by a purely personal relation to the individual. But once more we must realize that nothing can take place except

according to Law, and therefore this specific relation is nothing arbitrary, but arises out of the generic Law applied under specific conditions. And
since what makes a law generic is precisely the
fact that it does not supply the specific conditions,
it follows that the conditions for the specialising of
the Law must be provided by the individual. Then
it is that his recognition of the originating creative
movement, as arising from combined Thought and
Feeling, becomes a practical working asset. He
realizes that there is a Heart and Mind of the
Spirit reciprocal to his own heart and mind, that he
is not dealing with a filmy abstraction, nor yet with
a mere mathematical sequence, but with something
that is pulsating with a Life as warm and vivid and
full of interest as his own—nay, more so, for it is
the Infinite of all that he himself is. And his recognition goes even further than this, for since this
specialization can only take place through the individual himself, it logically follows that the Life,
which he thus specializes, become *his own* life.
Quoad the individual it does not know itself apart
from him. But this self-recognition through the
individual cannot in any way change the inherent
nature of the Creative Spirit, and therefore to the
extent to which the individual perceives its identi-
fication with himself, he places himself under its
guidance, and so he becomes one of those who are

"led by the Spirit." Thus he begins to find the Alpha and Omega of the Divine ideal reproduced in himself—in a very small degree at present, but containing the principle of perpetual growth into an infinite expansion of which we can as yet form no conception.

St. John sums up the whole of this position in his memorable words:—" Beloved now are we the Sons of God, and it doth not yet appear what we *shall* be; but we know that when He shall appear (*i.e.,* become clear to us) we shall be like Him; for (*i.e.,* the reason of all this) we shall see Him as He is " (I. John iii. 2).

THE CREATIVE POWER OF THOUGHT.

ONE of the great axioms in the new order of ideas, of which I have spoken, is that our Thought possesses creative power, and since the whole superstructure depends on this foundation, it is well to examine it carefully. Now the starting point is to see that Thought, or purely mental action, is the only possible source from which the existing creation could ever have come into manifestation at all, and it is on this account that in the preceding addresses I have laid stress on the origin of the cosmos. It is therefore not necessary to go over this ground again, and we will start this morning's enquiry on the assumption that every manifestation is in essence the expression of a Divine Thought. This being so, our own mind is the expression of a Divine Thought. The Divine Thought has produced something which itself is capable of thinking; but the question is whether its thinking has the same creative quality as that of the Parent Mind.

Now by the very hypothesis of the case the whole Creative Process consists in the continual pressing

50

forward of the Universal Spirit for expression through the individual and particular, and Spirit in its different modes is therefore the Life and Substance of the universe. Hence it follows that if there is to be an expression of thinking power it can only be by expressing the same thinking power which subsists latent in the Originating Spirit. If it were less than this it would only be some sort of mechanism and would not be thinking power, so that to be thinking power at all it must be identical in kind with that of the Originating Spirit. It is for this reason that man is said to be created in the image and likeness of God; and if we realize that it is impossible for him to be otherwise, we shall find a firm foundation from which to draw many important deductions.

But if our thought possesses this creative power, why are we hampered by adverse conditions? The answer is, because hitherto we have used our power invertedly. We have taken the starting point of our thought from external facts and consequently created a repetition of facts of a similar nature, and so long as we do this we must needs go on perpetuating the old circle of limitation. And, owing to the sensitiveness of the subconscious mind to suggestion—(See Edinburgh Lectures, chapter V.)—we are subject to a very powerful negative influence from those who are unacquainted with affirmative principles, and thus race-beliefs and the thought-currents of our more immediate environment tend to consolidate our own inverted thinking. It is therefore not surprising that the creative power of our thought, thus used in a wrong direction, has produced the limitations of which we complain. The remedy, then, is by reversing our method of thinking, and instead of taking external facts as our starting point, taking the inherent nature of mental power as our starting point. We have already gained two great steps in this direction, first by seeing that the whole manifested cosmos could have had its origin nowhere but in mental power, and secondly by realizing that our own mental power must be the same in kind with that of the Originating Mind.

Now we can go a step further and see how this power in ourselves can be perpetuated and intensified. By the nature of the creative process your mind is itself a thought of the Parent Mind; so, as long as this thought of the Universal Mind subsists, *you* will subsist, for you *are* it. But so long as you think this thought it continues to subsist, and necessarily remains present in the Divine Mind, thus fulfilling the logical conditions required for the perpetuation of the individual life. A poor analogy of the process may be found in a self-influencing dynamo where the magnetism generates the current and the current intensifies the magnetism with the result of producing a still stronger current until the limit of saturation is reached; only in the substantive infinitude of the Universal Mind and the potential infinitude of the Individual Mind there is no limit of saturation. Or we may compare the interaction of the two minds to two mirrors, a great and a small one, opposite each other, with the word "Life" engraved on the large one. Then, by the law of reflection, the word "Life" will also appear on the image of the smaller mirror reflected in the greater. Of course these are only very imperfect analogies; but if you can once grasp the idea of your own individuality as a thought in the Divine Mind which is able to perpetuate itself by thinking of itself as the thought which it is, you have got at the root of the whole matter, and by the same process you will not only perpetuate your life but will also expand it.

When we realize this on the one hand, and on the other that all external conditions, including the body, are produced by thought, we find ourselves standing between two infinites, the infinite of Mind and the infinite of Substance—from both of which we can draw what we will, and mould specific conditions out of the Universal Substance by the Creative Power which we draw in from the Universal Mind. But we must recollect that this is not by the force of personal will upon the substance, which is an error that will land us in all sorts of inversion, but by realizing our mind as a channel through which the Universal Mind operates upon substances in a particular way, according to the mode of thought which we are seeking to embody. If, then, our thought is habitually concentrated upon principles rather than on particular things, realizing that principles are nothing else than the Divine Mind in operation, we shall find that they will necessarily germinate to produce their own expression in corresponding facts, thus verifying the words of the Great Teacher, " Seek ye first the Kingdom of God and His righteousness and all these things shall be added unto you."

But we must never lose sight of the reason for the creative power of our thought, that it is because our mind is itself a thought of the Divine Mind, and that consequently our increase in livingness and creative power must be in exact proportion to our perception of our relation to the Parent Mind. In such considerations as these is to be found the philosophical basis of the Bible doctrine of " Sonship," with its culmination in the conception of the Christ. These are not mere fancies but the expression of strictly scientific principles, in their application to the deepest problems of the individual life; and their basis is that each one's world, whether in or out of the flesh, must necessarily be created by his own consciousness, and, in its turn, his mode of consciousness will necessarily take its colour from his conception of his relation to the Divine Mind—to the exclusion of light and colour, if he realizes no Divine Mind, and to their building up into forms of beauty in proportion as he realizes his identity of being with that All-Originating Spirit which is Light, Love, and Beauty in itself. Thus the great creative work of Thought in each of us is to make us consciously " sons and daughters of the Almighty," realizing that by our divine origin we can never be really separated from the Parent Mind which is continually seeking expression through us, and that any apparent separation is due to our own misconception of the true nature of the inherent relation between the Universal and the Individual. This is the lesson which the Great Teacher has so luminously put before us in the parable of the Prodigal Son.

THE GREAT AFFIRMATIVE.

THE Great Affirmative appears in two modes, the cosmic and the individual. In its essence it is the same in both, but in each it works from a different standpoint. It is always the principle of Being— that which *is*, as distinguished from that which is not; but to grasp the true significance of this saying we must understand what is meant by " that which is not." It is something more than mere non-existence, for obviously we should not trouble ourselves about what is non-existent. It is that which both is and is not at the same time, and the thing that answers to this description is " Conditions." The little affirmative is that which affirms particular conditions as all that it can grasp, while the great affirmative grasps a wider conception, the conception of that which gives rise to conditions. Cosmically it is that power of Spirit which sends forth the whole creation as its expression of itself, and it is for this reason that I have drawn attention in the preceding lectures to the idea of the creation *ex nihilo* of the whole visible universe. As Eastern and Western Scriptures alike tell us it is the breath-

ing-forth of Original Spirit; and if you have followed what I have said regarding the reproduction
of this Spirit in the individual—that by the very
nature of the creative process the human mind
must be of the same quality with the Divine Mind
—then we find that a second mode of the Originating Spirit becomes possible, namely that of operation through the individual mind. But whether
acting cosmically or personally it is always the
same Spirit and therefore cannot lose its inherent
character which is that of the Power which creates
ex nihilo. It is the direct contradiction of the
maxim " ex nihilo nihil fit "—nothing can be made
out of nothing; and it is the recognition of the
presence in ourselves of this power, which can make
something out of nothing, that is the key to our
further progress. As the logical outcome of the
cosmic creative process, the evolutionary work
reaches a point where the Originating Power creates an image of itself; and thus affords a fresh
point of departure from which it can work specifi-
cally, just as in the cosmic process it works gener-
ically. From this new standpoint it does not in
any way contradict the laws of the cosmic order,
but proceeds to specialize them, and thus to bring
out results through the individual which could not
be otherwise attained.

Now the Spirit does this by the same method as

in the Original Creation, namely by creating *ex nihilo;* for otherwise it would be bound by the limitations necessarily inherent in the cosmic *form* of things, and so no fresh creative starting point would have been attained. This is why the Bible lays such stress on the principle of Monogenesis, or creation from a single power instead of from a pair or syzegy; and it is on this account that we are told that this One-ness of God is the foundation of all the commandments, and that the " Son of God " is declared to be " monogenes " or one-begotten, for that is the correct translation of the Greek word. The immense importance of this principle of creation from a single power will become apparent as we realize more fully the results proceeding from the assumption of the opposite principle, or the dualism of the creative power; but as the discussion of this great subject would require a volume to itself, I must, at present, content myself with saying that this insistence of the Bible upon the singleness of the Creative Power is based upon a knowledge which goes to the very root of esoteric principles, and is therefore not to be set aside in favour of dualistic systems, though superficially the latter may appear more consonant to reason.

If, then, it is possible to put the Great Affirmation into words it is that God is ONE and that this ONE finds centre in ourselves; and if the full meaning of this statement is realized, the logical result will be found to be a new creation both in and from ourselves. We shall realize in ourselves the working of a new principle whose distinguishing feature is its simplicity. It is ONE-ness and is not troubled about any second. Hence what it contemplates is not how its action will be modified by that of some second principle, something which will compel it to work in a particular manner and so limit it; but what it contemplates is its own Unity. Then it perceives that its Unity consists in a greater and a lesser movement, just as the rotation of the earth on its axis does not interfere with its rotation round the sun but are both motions of the same unit, and are definitely related to each other. In like manner we find that the Spirit is moving simultaneously in the macrocosm of the universe and in the microcosm of the individual, and the two movements harmonize because they are that of the same Spirit, and the latter is included in the former, and pre-supposes it. The Great Affirmation, therefore, is the perception that the " I AM " is ONE, always harmonious with itself, and including all things in this harmony for the simple reason that there is no second creative power; and when the individual realizes that this always-single power is the root of his own being, and therefore has centre in himself and finds expression through him, he learns to trust its singleness and the consequent harmony of its action *in* him with what it is doing *around* him. Then he sees that the affirmation " I and my Father are ONE " is a necessary deduction from a correct apprehension of the fundamental principles of being; and then, on the principle that the less must be included in the greater, he desires that harmonious unity of action be maintained by the adaptation of his own particular movement to the larger movement of the Spirit working as the Creative Principle through the great whole. In this way we become centres through which the creative forces find specialization by the development of that personal factor on which the specific application of general laws must always depend. A specific sort of individuality is formed, capable of being the link between the great Spiritual Power of the universal and the manifestation of the relative in time and space because it consciously partakes of both; and because the individual of this class recognizes the singleness of the Spirit as the starting point of all things, he endeavours to withdraw his mind from all arguments derived from external conditions, whether past or present, and to fix it upon the forward movement of the Spirit which he knows to be always identical both in the universe and in himself. He ceases the attempt to dictate to the Spirit, because he does not see in it a mere blind force, but reveres it as the Supreme Intelligence: and on the other hand he does not grovel before it in doubt and fear, because he knows it is one with himself and is realizing itself through him, and therefore cannot have any purpose antagonistic to his own individual welfare. Realizing this he deliberately places his thoughts under the guidance of the Divine Spirit, knowing that his outward acts and conditions must thereby be brought into harmony with the great forward movement of the Spirit, not only at the stage he has now reached, but at all future stages. He does not at all deny the power of his own thought as the creative agent in his own personal world,—on the contrary it is precisely on the knowledge of this fact that his perception of the true adjustment between the principles of Life is based; but for this very reason he is the more solicitous to be led by that Wisdom which can see what he cannot see, so that his personal control over the conditions of his own life may be employed to its continual increase and development.

In this way our affirmation of the " I am " ceases to be the petulant assertion of our limited personality and becomes the affirmation that the Great I AM affirms its own I AM-ness both in us and through us, and thus our use of the words becomes in very truth the Great Affirmative, or that which is the root of all being as distinguished from that which has no being in itself but is merely externalized by being as the vehicle for its expression. We shall realize our true place as subordinate creative centres, perfectly independent of existing conditions because the creative process is that of monogenesis and requires no other factor than the Spirit for its exercise, but at the same time subordinate to the Divine Spirit in the greatness of its inherent forward movement because there is only ONE Spirit and it cannot from one centre antagonize what it is doing from another. Thus the Great Affirmation makes us children of the Great King, at once living in obedience to that Power which is above us, and exercising this same power over all that world of secondary causation which is below us.

Thus in our measure and station each one of us will receive the mission of the I AM.

CHRIST THE FULFILLING OF THE LAW.

"Think not that I am come to destroy the law or the prophets: I am not come to destroy but to fulfil." (Matt. v. 17.)

"Christ is the end of the law for righteousness to everyone that believeth." (Rom. x. 4.)

IF these words are the utterance of a mere sectarian superstition they are worthless; but if they are the statement of a great principle, then it is worth our while to enquire what that principle is. The fulfilling of anything is the bringing into complete realization of all that it potentially contains, and so the filling of any law to its fulness means bringing out all the possibilities which are hidden in it. This is precisely the method which has brought forth all the advances of material civilization. The laws of nature are the same now that they were in the days of our rugged Anglo-Saxon ancestors, but they brought out only an infinitesimal fraction of the possibilities which those laws contain : now we have brought out a good deal more, but we have by no means exhausted them, and so we continue to advance, not by contradicting natural laws, but by more fully realizing their capacity. Why should we not, then, apply the same method to ourselves and see whether there are no potentialities hidden away in the law of our own being which we have not as yet by any means brought to their fulfilment? We talk of a good time coming and of the ameliorating of the race; but do we reflect that the race is composed of individuals and that therefore real advance is to be made only by individual improvement, and not by Act of Parliament? and if so, then the individual with whom to begin is ourself.

The complete manifestation of the Law of Individuality is the end or purpose of the Bible teaching concerning Christ. It is a teaching based upon Law, spiritual and mental, fully recognizing that no effect can be produced except by the operation of an adequate cause; and Christ is set before us both as explaining the causes and exhibiting the full measure of the effects. All this is according to Law; and the importance of its being according to Law is that Law is universal, and the potentialities of the Law are therefore inherent in everyone—there is no special law for anybody, but anybody can specialize the law by using it with a fuller understanding of how much can be got out of it; and the purpose of the Scripture teaching regarding Christ is to help us to do this.

The preceding lectures have led us step by step

to see that the Originating Spirit, which first brought the world into existence, is also the root of our own individuality, and is therefore always ready, by its inherent nature, to continue the creative process from this individual stand-point as soon as the necessary conditions are provided, and these conditions are thought-conditions. Then by realizing the relation of Christ to the Originating Mind, the Parent Spirit or " Father," we receive a *standard* of thought which is bound to act creatively bringing out all the potentialities of our hidden being. Now the relation of Christ to the " Father " is that of the Architypal Idea in the All-creating Mind of which I have previously spoken, and so we arrive at the conception of the Christ-idea as a universal principle, and as being an idea therefore capable of reproduction in the individual Mind, thus explaining St. Paul's meaning when he speaks of Christ being formed in us. It is here that the principle of monogenesis comes in, that principle which I have endeavoured to describe in the earlier part of the present series as originating the whole manifested creation by an internal action of the Spirit upon itself; and it is the entire absence of control by any second power that renders the realization in external actuality of a purely mental ideal possible. For this reason systematic spiritual study commences with the contemplation of the existing cosmos, and we then transfer the conception of the monogenetic power of the Spirit from the cosmos to the individual and realize that the same Spirit is able to do the same thing in ourselves. This is the New Thought which in time will fulfil itself in the New Order, and we thus provide new thought-conditions which enable the Spirit to carry on its creative work from a new stand-point, that of our own individuality. This attainment by the Spirit of a new starting-point is what is meant by the esoteric doctrine of the Octave. The Octave is the starting-point of a new series reduplicating the starting-point of the previous series at a different level, just as does the octave note in music. We find this principle constantly referred to in Scripture—the completion of a prior series in the number Seven, and the starting of a new series by the number Eight, which takes the same place in the second series that the number One did in the first. The second series comes out of the first by natural growth and could not come into existence without it, hence the First or Originating number of the second series is the Eighth if we regard the second series as the prolongation of the first. Seven is the numerical correspondence of complete manifestation because it is the combination of three and four, which respectively represent the complete working of the spiritual and material factors—involution and evolution—and thus together constitute the finished whole. Students of the Tarot will here realize the process by which the Yod of Yod becomes the Yod of He. It is for this reason that the primary or cosmic creation terminates in the rest of the Seventh Day, for it can proceed no further until a fresh starting-point is found. But when this fresh starting-point is found in Man realizing his relation to the " Father," we start a new series and strike the Creative Octave and therefore the Resurrection takes place, not on the Sabbath or Seventh Day, but on the Eighth day which then becomes the First day of the new creative week. The *principle* of the Resurrection is the realization by man of his individualization of the Spirit and his recognition of the fact that, since the Spirit is always the same Spirit, it becomes the Alpha of a new creation from his own centre of being.

Now all this is necessarily an interior process taking place on the mental plane; but if we realize that the creative process is always primarily one of involution, or formation in the spiritual world, we shall grasp something of the meaning of Christ as " The Son of God "—the concentration of the Universal Spirit into a Personality on the spiritual plane correlatively to the individuality of each one who affords the necessary thought-conditions. To all who apprehend it there is then discovered in the

Universal Spirit the presence of a Divine Individuality reciprocal to that of the individual man, the recognition of which is the practical solution of all metaphysical problems regarding the emanation of the individual soul from the Universal Spirit and the relations arising therefrom; for it takes these matters out of the region of intellectual speculation, which is never creative but only analytical, and transfers it to the region of feeling and spiritual sensation which is the abode of the creative forces. This personal recognition of the Divine then affords us a new basis of Affirmation, and we need no longer trouble to go further back in order to analyze it, because we know experimentally that it is there; so now we find the starting-point of the new creation ready-made for us according to the architypal pattern in the Divine Mind itself and therefore perfectly correctly formed. When once this truth is clearly apprehended, whether we reach it by an intellectual process or by simple intuition, we can make it our starting-point and claim to have our thought permeated by the creative power of the Spirit on this basis.

But vast as is the conception thus reached we must remember that it is still a starting-point. It, indeed, transcends our previous range of ideas and so presents a culmination of the cosmic creative series which passes beyond that series and thus brings us to number Eight or the Octave; but on this very account it is the number One of a new creative series which is personal to the individual.

Then, because the Spirit is always the same, we may look for a repetition of the creative process at a higher level, and, as we all know, that process consists first of the involution of Spirit into Substance, and consequently of the subsequent evolution of Substance into forms continually increasing in fitness as vehicles for Spirit: so now we may look for a repetition of this universal process from its new starting-point in the individual mind and expect a corresponding externalization in accordance with our familiar axiom that thoughts are things.

Now it is as such an external manifestation of the Divine ideal that the Christ of the Gospels is set before us. I do not wish to dogmatize, but I will only say that the more clearly we realize the nature of the creative process on the spiritual side the more the current objections to the Gospel narrative lose their force; and it appears to me that to deny that narrative as a point-blank impossibility is to make a similar affirmation with regard to the power of the Spirit in ourselves. You cannot affirm a principle and deny it in the same breath; and if we affirm the externalizing power of the Spirit in our own case, I do not see how we can logically lay down a limit for its action and say that under highly specialized conditions it could not produce highly specialized effects. It is for this reason that St. John puts the question of Christ manifest in the flesh as the criterion of the whole matter (I. John iv., 2). If the Spirit can create at all then you cannot logically limit the extent or method of its working; and since the basis of our expectation of individual expansion is the limitless creative power of the Spirit, to reject the Christ of the Gospels as an impossibility is to cut away the ground from under our own feet. It is one thing to say " I do not understand why the Spirit should have worked in that way "—that is merely an honest statement of our present stage of knowledge, or we may even go the length of saying that we do not feel convinced that it did work in that way—that is a true confession of our intellectual difficulty—but certainly those who are professedly relying on the power of the Spirit to produce external results cannot say that it does not possess that power, or possesses it only in a limited degree: the position is logically self-destructive. What we should do therefore, is to suspend judgment and follow the light as far as we can see it, and bye-and-bye it will become clearer to us. There are, it appears to me, occult heights in the doctrine of Christ designed by the Supreme Wisdom to counteract corresponding occult depths in the Mystery of Darkness. I do not think it is at all necessary, or even possible, for us to scale these heights or fathom those depths, with our present infantile intelligence, but if we realize how completely the law of our being receives its fulfilment in Christ as far as we know that law, may we not well conceive that there are yet deeper phases of that law the existence of which we can only faintly surmise by intuition? Occasionally just the fringe of the veil is lifted for some of us, but that momentary glance is enough to show us that there are powers and mysteries beyond our present conception. But even there Law reigns supreme, and therefore taking Christ as our basis and starting-point, we start with the Law already fulfilled, whether in those things which are familiar to us or in those realms which are beyond our thought, and so we need have no fear of evil. Our starting-point is that of a divinely ordained security from which we may quietly grow into that higher evolution which is the fulfilment of the law of our own being.

THE STORY OF EDEN.

THE whole Bible and the whole history of the world, past, present and future, are contained in embryo in the story of Eden, for they are nothing else than the continuous unfolding of certain great principles which are there allegorically stated. That this is by no means a new notion is shown by the following quotation from Origen:—" Who is there so foolish and without common-sense as to believe that God planted trees in the Garden of Eden like a husbandman; and planted therein the tree of life perceptible to the eyes and to the senses, which gave life to the eater; and another tree which gave to the eater a knowledge of good and evil? I believe that everybody must regard these as figures under which a recondite sense is concealed." Let us, then, follow up the suggestion of this early Father of the Church, and enquire what may be the " recondite sense " concealed under this figure of the two trees. On the face of the story there are two roots, one of Life and the other of Death, two fundamental principles bring-ing about diametrically opposite results. The dis-

72

tinctive mark of the latter is that it is the knowledge of good and evil, that is to say, the recognition of two antagonistic principles, and so requiring a knowledge of the relations between them to enable us to continually make the needful adjustments to keep ourselves going. Now, in appearance this is exceedingly specious. It looks so entirely reasonable that we do not see its ultimate destructiveness; and so we are told that Eve ate the fruit because she " saw that the tree was pleasant to the eyes." But careful consideration will show us in what the destructive nature of this principle consists. It is based on the fallacy that good is limited by evil, and that you cannot receive any good except through eliminating the corresponding evil by realizing it and beating it back. In this view life becomes a continual combat against every imaginable form of evil, and after we have racked our brains to devise precautions against all possible evil happenings, there remains the chance, and much more than the chance, that we have by no means exhausted the category of negative possibilities, and that others may arise which no amount of foresight on our part could have imagined. The more we see into this position the more intolerable it becomes, because from this stand-point we can never attain any certain basis of action, and the forces of possible evil multiply as we contemplate them. To set forth to out-wit all evil by our own knowledge of its nature is to attempt a task the hopelessness of which becomes apparent when we see it in its true light.

The mistake is in supposing that Life can be generated in ourselves by an intellectual process; but, as we have seen in the preceding lectures, Life is the primary movement of the Spirit, whether in the cosmos or in the individual. In its proper order intellectual knowledge is exceedingly important and useful, but its place in the order of the whole is not that of the Originator. It is not Life in itself, but is a function of life; it is an effect and not the cause. The reason why this is so is because intellectual study is always the study of the various laws which arise from the different *relations* of things to one another; and it therefore presupposes that these things together with their laws are already in existence. Consequently it does not start from the truly creative stand-point, that of creating something entirely new, creation *ex nihilo* as distinguished from *construction*, or the laying-together of existing materials, which is what the word literally means. To recognize evil as a force to be reckoned with is therefore to give up the creative stand-point altogether. It is to quit the plane of First Cause and descend into the realm of secondary causation and lose ourselves amid the confusion of a multiplicity of relative causes and effects without grasping any unifying principle behind them.

Now the only thing that can release us from the inextricable confusion of an infinite multiplicity is the realization of an underlying unity, and at the back of all things we find the presence of one Great Affirmative principle without which nothing could have existence. This, then, is the Root of Life; and if we credit it with being able, not only to supply the power, but also the form for its manifestation we shall see that we need not go beyond this *single* Power for the production of anything. It is Spirit producing Substance out of its own essence, and the Substance taking Form in accordance with the movement of the Spirit. What we have to realize is, not only that this is the way in which the cosmos is brought into existence, but also that, because the Spirit finds a new centre in ourselves, the same process is repeated in our own mentality, and therefore we are continually creating *ex nihilo* whether we know it or not. Consequently, if we look upon evil as a force to be reckoned with, and therefore requiring to be studied, we are in effect creating it; while on the other hand if we realize that there is only *one* force to be considered, and that absolutely good, we are by the law of the creative process bringing that good into manifestation. No doubt for this affirmative use of our creative power it is necessary that we start from the basic conception of a *single* originating power which is absolutely good and life-giving; but if there were a self-originating power which was destructive then no creation could ever have come into existence at all, for the positive and negative self-originating powers would cancel each other and the result would be zero. The fact, therefore, of our own existence is a sufficient proof of the singleness and goodness of the Originating Power, and from this starting-point there is no second power to be taken into consideration, and consequently we do not have to study the evil that may arise out of existing or future circumstances, but require to keep our minds fixed only upon the good which we intend to create. There is a very simple reason for this. It is that every new creation necessarily carries its own law with it and by that law produces new conditions of its own. A balloon affords a familiar illustration of my meaning. The balloon with its freight weighs several hundredweight, yet the introduction of a new factor, the gas, brings with it a law of its own which entirely alters the conditions, and the force of gravity is so completely overcome that the whole mass rises into the air. The Law itself is never altered, but we have previously known it only under limiting conditions. These conditions, however, are no part of the Law itself; and a clearer realization of the Law shows us that it contains in itself the power of transcending them. The law which every new creation carries with it is therefore not a contradiction of the old law but its specialization into a higher mode of action.

Now the ultimate Law is that of production *ex nihilo* by the movement of the Spirit within itself, and all subordinate laws are merely the measurements of the relations which spontaneously arise between different things when they are brought into manifestation, and therefore, if an entirely new thing is created it must necessarily establish entirely new relations and so produce entirely new laws. This is the reason why, if we take the action of pure unmanifested Spirit as our starting-point, we may confidently trust it to produce manifestations of law which, though perfectly new from the stand-point of our past experience, are quite as natural in their own way as any that have gone before. It is on this account that in these addresses I lay so much stress on the fact that Spirit creates *ex nihilo*, that is, out of no pre-existing forms, but simply by its own movement within itself. If, then, this idea is clearly grasped, it logically follows from it that the Root of Life is not to be found in the comparison of good and evil, but in the simple affirmation of the Spirit as the All-creating power of Good. And since, as we have already seen, this same all-creating Spirit finds a centre and fresh starting-point of operation in our own minds, we can trust it to follow the Law of its own being there as much as in the creation of the cosmos.

Only we must not forget that it is working through our own minds. It thinks through our mind, and our mind must be made a suitable channel for this mode of its operation by conforming itself to the broad generic lines of the Spirit's thinking. The reason for this is one which I have sought to impress throughout these lectures, namely, that the specialization of a law is never the denial of it, but on the contrary the fuller recognition of its basic principles; and if this is the case in ordinary physical science it must be equally so when we come to specialize the great Law of Life itself. The Spirit can never change its essential nature as the essence of Life, Love, and Beauty; and if we adopt these characteristics, which constitute the Law of the Spirit, as the basis of our own thinking, and reject all that is contrary to them, then we afford the broad generic conditions for the specialized thinking of the Spirit through our own minds: and the thinking of the Spirit is that *involution*, or passing of spirit into form, which is the whole being of the creative process.

The mind which is all the time being thus formed

is our own. It is not a case of control by an external individuality, but the fuller expression of the Universal through an organized mentality which has all along been a less perfect expression of the Universal; and therefore the process is one of growth. We are not losing our individuality, but are coming into fuller possession of ourselves by the conscious recognition of our personal share in the great work of creation. We begin in some slight measure to understand what the Bible means when it speaks of our being "partakers of the Divine nature" (II. Peter i. 4) and we realize the significance of the "unity of the Spirit" (Ephesians iv. 3). Doubtless this will imply changes in our old mode of thinking; but these changes are not forced upon us, they are brought about naturally by the new stand-point from which we now see things. Almost imperceptibly to ourselves we grow into a New Order of Thought which proceeds, not from a knowledge of good and evil, but from the Principle of Life itself. That is what makes the difference between our old thought and our new thought. Our old thought was based upon a comparison of limited facts: our new thought is based upon a comprehension of principles. The difference is like that between the mathematics of the infant, who cannot count beyond the number of apples or marbles put before him, and that of the senior wrangler who is not dependent upon visible objects for his calculations, but plunges boldly into the unknown because he knows that he is working by indubitable principles. In like manner when we realize the infallible Principle of the Creative Law we no longer find we need to see everything cut and dried beforehand, for if so, we could never get beyond the range of our old experiences; but we can move steadily forward because we know the certainty of the creative principle by which we are working, or rather, which is working through us, and that our life, in all its minutest details, is its harmonious expression. Thus the Spirit thinks through our thought only its thought is greater than ours. It is the paradox of the less containing the greater. Our thought will not be objectless or unintelligible to ourselves. It will be quite clear as far as it goes. We shall know exactly what we want to do and why we want to do it, and so will act in a reasonable and intelligent manner. But what we do not know is the greater thought that is all the time giving rise to our smaller thought, and which will open out from it as our lesser thought progresses into form. Then we gradually see the greater thought which prompted our small-er one and we find ourselves working along its lines, guided by the invisible hand of the Creative Spirit into continually increasing degrees of livingness to which we need assign no limits, for it is the expansion of the Infinite within ourselves.

This, as it appears to me, is the hidden meaning of the two trees in Eden, the Garden of the Soul. It is the distinction between a knowledge which is merely that of comparisons between different sorts of conditions, and a knowledge which is that of the Life which gives rise to and therefore controls conditions. Only we must remember that the control of conditions is not to be attained by violent self-assertion which is only recognizing them as substantive entities to be battled with, but by conscious unity with that All-creating Spirit which works silently, but surely, on its own lines of Life, Love, and Beauty.

" Not by might, nor by power, but by My Spirit, saith the Lord of Hosts."

THE WORSHIP OF ISHI.

In Hosea ii. 16 we find this remarkable statement:—" And it shall be at that day, saith the Lord, that thou shalt call Me Ishi, and shalt no more call Me Baali "; and with this we may couple the statement in Isaiah lxii. 4:—" Thou shalt be called Hephzibah, and thy land Beulah; for the Lord delighteth in thee, and thy land shall be married."

In both these passages we find a change of name; and since a name stands for something which corresponds to it, and in truth only amounts to a succinct description, the fact indicated in these texts is a change of condition answering to the change of name.

Now the change from Baali to Ishi indicates an important alteration in the relation between the Divine Being and the worshipper; but since the Divine Being cannot change, the altered relation must result from a change in the stand-point of the worshipper: and this can only come from a new mode of looking at the Divine, that is, from a new order of thought regarding it. Baali means Lord, and Ishi means husband, and so the change in relation is that of a female slave who is liberated and married to her former master. We could not have a more perfect analogy. Relatively to the Universal Spirit the individual soul is esoterically feminine, as I have pointed out in " Bible Mystery and Bible Meaning," because its function is that of the receptive and formative. This is necessarily inherent in the nature of the creative process. But the individual's development as the specializing medium of the Universal Spirit will depend entirely upon his own conception of his relation to it. So long as he only regards it as an arbitrary power, a sort of slave owner, he will find himself in the position of a slave driven by an inscrutable force, he knows not whither or for what purpose. He may worship such a God, but his worship is only the worship of fear and ignorance, and there is no personal interest in the matter except to escape some dreaded punishment. Such a worshipper would gladly escape from his divinity, and his worship, when analyzed, will be found to be little else than disguised hatred. This is the natural result of a worship based upon *unexplained* traditions instead of intelligible principles, and is the very opposite of that worship in Spirit and in truth which Jesus speaks of as the true worship.

But when the light begins to break in upon us, all this becomes changed. We see that a system of terrorism cannot give expression to the Divine Spirit, and we realize the truth of St. Paul's words,

" He hath not given us the spirit of fear, but of power, and of love, and of a sound mind." As the true nature of the relation between the individual mind and the Universal Mind becomes clearer, we find it to be one of mutual action and re-action, a perfect reciprocity which cannot be better symbolized than by the relation between an affectionate husband and wife. Everything is done from love and nothing from compulsion, there is perfect confidence on both sides, and both are equally indispensable to each other. It is simply the carrying out of the fundamental maxim that the Universal cannot act on the plane of the Particular except through the Particular; only this philosophical axiom develops into a warm living intercourse.

Now this is the position of the soul which is indicated by the name Hephzibah. In common with all other words derived from the Semitic root " hafz " it implies the idea of guarding, just as in the East a *hafiz* is one who guards the letter of the Koran by having the whole book by heart, and in many similar expressions. Hephzibah may therefore be translated as " a guarded one," thus recalling the New Testament description of those who are " guarded into salvation." It is precisely this conception of being guarded by a superior power that distinguishes the worship of Ishi from that of Baali. A special relation has been established between the Divine Spirit and the individual soul, one of abso-

lute confidence and personal intercourse. This
does not require any departure from the general
law of the universe, but is due to that specializing
of the law through the presentation of special conditions personal to the individual, of which I have
spoken before. But all the time there has been no
change in the Universal Spirit, the only change has
been in the mental attitude of the individual—he
has come into a new thought, a clearer perception
of God. He has faced the questions, What is God?
Where is God? How does God work? and he has
found the answer in the apostolic statement that
God is " over all, through all, and in all," and he
realises that " God " is the root of his (the individual's) own being, ever present *in* him, ever
working *through* him, and universally present around
him.

This realization of the true relation between the
Originating Spirit and the individual mind is what
is esoterically spoken of as the Mystical Marriage
in which the two have ceased to be separate and
have become one. As a matter of fact they always
were one, but since we can apprehend things only
from the stand-point of our own consciousness, it is
our recognition of the fact that makes it a practical
reality for ourselves. But an intelligent recognition
will never make a confusion of the two parts of
which the whole consists, and will never lead the
individual to suppose that he is handling a blind

force or that a blind force is handling him. He will neither dethrone God, nor lose himself by absorption in deity, but he will recognize the reciprocity of the Divine and the human as the natural and logical outcome of the essential conditions of the creative process.

And what is the Whole which is thus created? It is our conscious *personality ;* and therefore whatever we draw from the Universal Spirit acquires in us the quality of personality. It is that process of differentiation of the universal into the particular of which I have so often spoken, which, by a rude analogy, we may compare to the differentiation of the universal electric fluid into specific sorts of power by its passage through suitable apparatus. It is for this reason that relatively to ourselves the Universal Spirit must necessarily assume a personal aspect, and that the aspect which it will assume will be in exact correspondence with our own conception of it. This is in accordance with mental and spiritual laws inherent in our own being, and it is on this account that the Bible seeks to build up our conception of God on such lines as will set us free from all fear of evil, and thus leave us at liberty to use the creative power of our thought affirmatively from the stand-point of a calm and untroubled mind. This stand-point can only be reached by passing beyond the range of the happenings of the moment, and this can only be done by the discovery of our immediate relation to the undifferentiated source of all good. I lay stress on these words " immediate " and " undifferentiated " because in them is contained the secret of the whole position. If we could not draw immediately from the Universal Spirit our receiving would be subject to the limitations of the channel through which it reached us; and if the force which we receive were not undifferentiated in itself it could not take appropriate form in our own minds and become to each of us just what we require it to be. It is this power of the human soul to differentiate limitlessly from the Infinite that we are apt to overlook, but as we come to realize that the soul is itself a reflection and image of the Infinite Spirit—and a clear recognition of the cosmic creative process shows that it cannot be anything else—we find that it must possess this power, and that in fact it is our possession of this power which is the whole *raison d'etre* of the creative process: if the human soul did not possess an unlimited power of differentiation from the Infinite, then the Infinite would not be reflected in it, and consequently the Infinite Spirit would find no outlet for its *conscious* recognition of itself as the Life, Love, and Beauty which it is. We can never too deeply ponder the old esoteric definition of Spirit as " the Power which knows itself " : the secret of all things, past, present, and future is contained in these few words. The self-recognition or self-contemplation of Spirit is the primary movement out of which all creation proceeds, and the attainment in the individual of a fresh centre for self-recognition is what the Spirit *gains* in the process—this *gain* accruing to the Spirit is what is referred to in the parables where the lord is represented as receiving increase from his servants.

When the individual perceives this relation between himself and Infinite Spirit, he finds that he has been raised from a position of slavery to one of reciprocity. The Spirit cannot do without him any more than he can do without the Spirit : the two are as necessary to each other as the two poles of an electric battery. The Spirit is the unlimited essence of Love, Wisdom, and Power, all three in one undifferentiated and waiting to be differentiated by *appropriation*, that is, by the individual *claiming* to be the channel of their differentiation. It only requires the claim to be made with the recognition that by the Law of Being it is bound to be answered, and the right feeling, the right seeing, and the right working for the particular matter we have in hand will flow in quite naturally. Our old enemies, doubt and fear, may seek to bring us back under bondage to Baali, but our new stand-point for the recognition of the All-originating Spirit as being absolutely unified with ourselves must always be kept resolutely in mind; for, short of this, we are not working on the creative level—we are creating, indeed, for we can never divest ourselves of our creative power, but we are creating in the image of the old limiting and destructive conditions, and this is merely perpetuating the cosmic Law of Averages, which is just what the individual has to rise superior to. The creative level is where new laws begin to manifest themselves in a new order of conditions, something transcending our past experiences and thus bringing about a real advance; for it is no advance only to go on in the same old round even if we kept at it for centuries: it is the steady go-ahead nature of the Spirit that has made the world of to-day an improvement upon the world of the pterodactyl and the icthiosaurus, and we must look for the same forward movement of the Spirit from its new starting-point in ourselves.

Now it is this special, personal, and individual relation of the Spirit to ourselves which is typified by the names Ishi and Hephzibah. From this stand-point we may say that as the individual wakes up to the oneness with the Spirit, the Spirit wakes up to the same thing. It becomes conscious of itself through the consciousness of the individual, and thus is solved the paradox of individual self-recognition by the Universal Spirit, without which

no *new*-creative power could be exercised and all
things would continue to proceed in the old merely
cosmic order. It is of course true that in the
merely generic order the Spirit must be present in
every form of Life, as the Master pointed out when
He said that not a sparrow falls to the ground
without " the Father." But as the sparrows He alluded to had been shot and were on sale at a price
which shows that this was the fate of a good many
of them, we see here precisely that stage of manifestation where the Spirit has not woke up to individual self-recognition, and remains at the lower
level of self-recognition, that of the generic or race-
spirit. The Master's comment, " Ye are of more
value than many sparrows " points out this difference : in us the generic creation has reached the
level which affords the conditions for the waking up
of the Spirit to self-recognition in the Individual.

And we must bear in mind that all this is perfectly natural. There is no posing or straining after
effect about it. If *you* have to pump up the Life,
who is going to put the Life into you to pump it?
Therefore it is spontaneous or nothing. That is
why the Bible speaks of it as the free gift of God.
It cannot be anything else. You cannot originate
the originating force; it must originate you : but
what you can do is to distribute it. Therefore immediately you experience any sense of friction be

sure there is something wrong somewhere; and since God can never change, you may be sure that the friction is being caused by some error in your own thinking—you are limiting the Spirit in some way : set to work to find out what it is. It is always *limiting* the Spirit that does this. You are tying it down to conditions somewhere, saying it is bound by reason of some existing forms. The remedy is to go back to the original starting point of the Cosmic Creation and ask, Where were the pre-existing forms that dictated to the Spirit then? Then because the Spirit never changes it is *still the same*, and is just as independent of existing conditions now as it was in the beginning; and so we must pass over all existing conditions, however apparently adverse, and go straight to the Spirit as the originator of new forms and new conditions. This is real New Thought, for it does not trouble about the old things, but is going straight ahead from where we are now. When we do this, just trusting the Spirit, and not laying down the particular details of its action—just telling it what we want without dictating *how* we are to get it—we shall find that things will open out more and more clearly day by day both on the inner and the outer plane. Remember that the Spirit is alive and working here and now, for if ever the Spirit is to get from the past into the future it must be by passing through the present; therefore what you have to do is to acquire the habit of living direct from the Spirit here and now. You will soon find that this is a matter of personal intercourse, perfectly natural and not requiring any abnormal conditions for its production. You just treat the Spirit as you would any other kind-hearted sensible person, remembering that it is always there—" closer than hands and feet," as Tennyson says—and you will gradually begin to appreciate its reciprocity as a very practical fact indeed.

This is the relation of Hephzibah to Ishi, and is that worship in Spirit and in truth which needs neither the temple in Jerusalem nor yet in Samaria for its acceptance, for the whole world is the temple of the Spirit and you yourself its sanctuary. Bear this in mind, and remember that nothing is too great or too small, too interior or too external, for the Spirit's recognition and operation, for the Spirit is itself both the Life and the Substance of all things and it is also Self-recognition from the stand-point of your own individuality; and therefore, because the Self-recognition of Spirit is the Life of the creative process, you will, by simply trusting the Spirit to work according to its own nature, pass more and more completely into that New Order which proceeds from the thought of Him who says, " Behold I make all things new."

THE SHEPHERD AND THE STONE.

THE metaphor of the Shepherd and the Sheep is of constant occurrence throughout the Bible and naturally suggests the idea of the guiding, guarding, and feeding both of the individual sheep and of the whole flock and it is not difficult to see the spiritual correspondence of these things in a general sort of way. But we find that the Bible combines the metaphor of the Shepherd with another metaphor that of " the Stone," and at first sight the two seem rather incongruous.

" From thence is the Shepherd the Stone of Israel," says the Old Testament (Genesis xlix. 24), and Jesus calls himself both " The Good Shepherd " and " The Stone which the builders rejected." The Shepherd and the Stone are thus identified and we must therefore seek the interpretation in some conception which combines the two. A shepherd suggests Personal care for the welfare of the sheep, and an intelligence greater than theirs. A stone suggests the idea of Building, and consequently of measurement, adaptation of parts to whole, and progressive construction according to plan. Com-

93

bining these two conceptions we get the idea of the building of an edifice whose stones are persons, each taking their more or less conscious part in the construction—thus a building, not constructed from without, but self-forming by a principle of growth from within under the guidance of a Supreme Wisdom permeating the whole and conducting it stage by stage to ultimate completeness. This points to a Divine Order in human affairs with which we may more or less consciously co-operate: both to our personal advantage and also to the further-ance of the great scheme of human evolution as a whole; the ultimate purpose being to establish in *all* men that principle of " The Octave " to which I have already alluded; and in proportion as some adumbration of this principle is realized by individu-als and by groups of individuals they specialize the law of race-development, even though they may not be aware of the fact, and so come under a *spe-cialized* working of the fundamental Law, which thus differentiates them from other individuals and nationalities, as by a peculiar guidance, producing higher developments which the merely generic op-eration of the Law could not.

Now if we keep steadily in mind that, though the purpose, or Law of Tendency, or the Originating Spirit must always be universal in its nature, it must necessarily be individual in its operation, we shall see that this universal purpose can only be accomplished through the instrumentality of specific means. This results from the fundamental proposition that the Universal can only work on the plane of the Particular by becoming the individual and particular; and when we grasp the conception that the merely generic operation of the Creative Law has now brought the human race as far as it can, that is to say it has completely evolved the merely natural *genus homo*, it follows that if any further development is to take place it can only be by the co-operation of the individual himself. Now it is the spread of this individual co-operation that the forward movement of the Spirit is leading us to, and it is the gradual extension of this universal principle that is alluded to in the prophecy of Daniel regarding the Stone cut out without hands that spreads until it fills the whole earth (Daniel ii. 34 and 44). According to the interpretation given by Daniel, this Stone is the emblem of a spiritual Kingdom, and the identity of the Stone and the Shepherd indicates that the Kingdom of the Stone must be also the Kingdom of the Shepherd; and the Master, who identified himself with both the Stone and the Shepherd, emphatically declared that this Kingdom was, in its essence, an interior Kingdom—"the Kingdom of Heaven is within you." We must look for its foundation therefore, in a spiritual principle or mental law inherent in the constitution of all men but waiting to be brought into fuller development by more accurate compliance with its essential requirements; which is precisely the method by which science has evoked powers from the laws of nature which were undreamt of in former ages; and in like manner the recognition of our true relation to the Universal Spirit, which is the source of all individual being, must lead to an advance both for the race and for the individual such as we can at present scarcely form the faintest idea of, but which we dimly apprehend through the intuition and speak of as the New Order. The approach of this New Order is everywhere making itself vaguely felt; it is, as the French say, in the air, and the very vagueness and mystery attending it is causing a feeling of unrest as to what form it may assume. But to the student of Spiritual Law this should not be the case. He knows that the Form is always the expression of the Spirit, and therefore, since he is in touch with the forward movement of the Spirit, he knows that he himself will always be harmoniously included in any form of development which the Great Forward Movement may take. This is the practical and personal benefit arising from the realization of the Principle which is symbolized under the two-fold metaphor of the Shepherd and the Stone. and in all those new developments which are perhaps even now within measurable distance, we can rest on the knowledge that we are under the care of a kind Shepherd, and under the formation of a wise Master Builder.

But the principle of the Shepherd and the Stone is not something hitherto unheard of which is only to come into existence in the future. If there were no manifestations of this principle in the past, we might question whether there were any such principle at all; but a careful study of the subject will show us that it has been at work all through the ages, sometimes in modes more immediately bearing the aspect of the Shepherd, and sometimes in modes more immediately bearing the aspect of the Stone, though the one always implies the other, for they are the same thing seen from different points of view. The subject is one of immense interest, but covering such a wide range of study that all I can do here is to point out that such a field of investigation exists and is worth exploration; and the exploration brings its reward with it, not only by putting us in possession of the key to the history of the past, but by showing us that it is the key to the history of the future also, and furthermore by making evident on a large scale the working of the same principle of Spiritual Law by co-operation with which we may facilitate the process of our own individual evolution. It thus adds a vivid interest to life, giving us something worth looking forward to and introducing us to a personal future which is not limited by the proverbial three-score years and ten.

Now, we have seen that the first stage in the Creative Process is always that of Feeling—a reaching-out by the Spirit in a particular direction, and therefore we may look for something of the same kind in the development of the great principle which we are now considering. And we find this first vague movement of this great principle in the intuitions of a particular race which appears from time immemorial to have combined the two characteristics of nomad wandering with their flocks and herds and the symbolization of their religious beliefs in monuments of stone. The monuments themselves have taken different forms in different countries and ages, but the identity of their symbolism becomes clear under careful investigation. Together with this symbolism we always find the nomad character of the builders and that they are invested with an aura of mystery and romance such as we find nowhere else, though we always find it surrounding these builders, even in countries so far apart as India and Ireland. Then, as we pass beyond the merely monumental stage, we find threads of historical evidence connecting the different branches of this race, increasing in their complexity and strengthening in their cumulative force as we go on, until at last we are brought to the history of the age in which we live; and finally most remarkable affinities of language put the finishing touch to the mass of proofs which can be gathered along all these different lines. In this magic circle countries so remote from one another as Ireland and Greece, Egypt and India, Palestine and Persia, are brought into close contiguity—a similar tradition, and even a similar nomenclature, unite the mysterious builders of the Great Pyramid with the equally mysterious builders of the Round Towers of Ireland—and the Great Pyramid itself, perhaps antedating the call of Abraham, re-appears as the official seal of the United States; while tradition traces the crowning-stone in Westminster Abbey back to the time of Solomon's temple and even earlier. For the most part the erewhile wanderers are now settled in their destined homes, but the Anglo-Saxon race—the People of the Corner-Stone—are still the pioneers among the nations, and there is something esoteric in the old joke that when the North Pole is reached a Scotchman will be found there. And not least in the chain of evidence is the link afforded by a tribe who are wanderers still, the Gipsies with their duplicate of the Pyramid in the pack of cards—a volume which has been called " The Devil's Picture Book " by those who know it only in its misuse and inversion, but which when interpreted in the light of the knowledge we are now gaining, affords a signal instance of that divine policy by which as St. Paul says, God employs the foolish things of this world to confute the wise; while a truer apprehension of the Gipsies themselves indicates their unmistakable connection with that race who through all its wanderings has ever been the guardian of the Stone.

In these few paragraphs I have only been able to point out very briefly the broad lines of enquiry into a subject of national importance to the British and American peoples, and which interests us personally, not only as members of these nations, but as affording proof on the largest scale of the same specialization of universal laws which each of us has to effect individually for ourself. But whether the process be individual or national it is always the same, and is the translation to the very highest plane—that of the All-originating Life itself—of the old maxim that " Nature will obey us exactly in proportion as we first obey Nature "; it is the old parable of the lord who, finding his servants girt and awaiting him, then girds himself and serves them (Luke xii. 35 to 37). The nation or the individual who thus realizes the true principle of the Shepherd and the Stone, comes under a special Divine guidance and protection, not by a favouritism incompatible with the conception of universal Law, but by the very operation of the Law itself. They have come into touch with its higher possibilities, and to recur to an analogy which I have already employed, they learn to make their iron float by the very same law by which it sinks; and so they become the flock of the Great Shepherd and the building of the Great Architect, and each one, however insignificant his or her sphere may appear, becomes a sharer in the great work, and by a logical consequence begins to grow on new lines of development for the simple reason that a new principle necessarily produces new modes of manifestation. If the reader will think over these things he will see that the promises contained in the Bible, whether national or personal, are nothing else than statements of the universal law of Cause and Effect applied to the inmost principles of our being, and that therefore it is not mere rhapsody, but the figurative expression of a great truth when the Psalmist says " The Lord is my Shepherd," and " Thou art my God and the Rock of my salvation."

SALVATION IS OF THE JEWS.

WHAT does this saying of the Master's mean? Certainly not a mere arrogant assumption in favour of His own nationality—such an idea is negatived, not only by the universality of all His other teaching, but also by the very instruction in which these words occur, for He declared that the Jewish temple was equally with the Samaritan of no account in the matter. He said that the true worship was purely spiritual and entirely independent of places and ceremonies, while at the same time He emphasized the Jewish expectation of a Messiah, so that in this teaching we are met by the paradox of a universal principle combined with what at first sight appears like a tribal tradition quite incompatible with any recognition of the universal reign of law. How to reconcile these apparent opposites, therefore, seems to be the problem which He here sets before us. Its solution is to be found in that principle which I have endeavoured to elucidate throughout these lectures, the specializing of universal law. Opinions may differ as to whether the Bible narrative of the birth of Christ is to be taken literally or symbolically, but as to the spiritual principle involved there can, I think, be no difference of opinion. It is that of the specialization by the individual of the generic relation of the soul to the Infinite Spirit from which it proceeds. The relation itself is universal and results from the very nature of the creative process, but the law of the universal relation admits of particular specialization exactly in the same way as all other natural laws— it is simpy applying to the supreme Law of Life the same method by which we have learnt to make iron float, that is to say by a fuller recognition of what the Law is in itself. Whatever other meanings we may apply to the name Messiah, it undoubtedly stands for the absolutely perfect manifestation in the individual of all the infinite possibilities of the Principle of Life.

Now it was because this grand ideal is the basis on which the Hebrew nationality was founded that Jesus made this statement. This foundation had been lamentably misconceived by the Jewish people; but nevertheless, however imperfectly, they still held by it, and from them this ideal has spread throughout the Christian world. Here also it continues to be lamentably misconceived, nevertheless it is still retained, and only needs to be recognized in its true light as a universal principle, instead of an unintelligible dogma, to become the salvation of the world. Hence, as affording the medium through which this supreme ideal has been preserved and spread, it is true that " Salvation is of the Jews."

Their fundamental idea was right but their apprehension of it was wrong—that is why the Master at the same time sweeps away the national worship of the temple and preserves the national idea of the Messiah; and this is equally true of the Christian world at the present day. If salvation is anything real it must have its cause in some law, and if there is a law it must be founded upon some universal principle: therefore it is this principle which we must seek if we would understand this teaching of the Master's.

Now whether we take the Bible story of the birth of Christ literally or symbolically, it teaches one great lesson. It teaches that the All-originating Spirit is the true Parent of the individual both in soul and body. This is nothing else than realizing from the stand-point of the individual what we cannot help realizing in regard to the original creation of the cosmos—it is the realization that the All-originating Spirit is at once the Life and the Substance in each individual here and now, just as it must have been in the origin of all things. Human parentage counts for nothing—it is only the channel through which Universal Spirit has acted for the concentration of an individual centre; but the ultimate cause of that centre, both in life and substance, continues at every moment to be the One same Originating Spirit.

This recognition cuts away the root of all the power of the negative, and so in principle it delivers us from all evil, for the root of evil is the denial of the power of the Spirit to produce good. When we realize that the Spirit is finding its own individualization in us in its two-fold essence as Life and Substance, then we see that it must be both able and willing to create for us all good. The only limit is that which we ourselves impose by denying its operation, and when we realize the inherent creativeness of Spirit we find that there is no reason why we should stop short at any point and say that it can go no further. Our error is in looking on the life of the body as separate from the life of the Spirit, and this error is met by the consideration that, in its ultimate nature, Substance must emanate from Spirit and is nothing else than the record of Spirit's conception of itself as finding expression in space and time. And when this becomes clear it follows that Substance need not be taken into calculation at all. The material form stands in the same relation to Spirit that the image projected on the screen stands to the slide in the lantern. If we wish to change the exhibited subject we do not manipulate the reflection on the screen, but we alter the slide; and in like manner, when we come to realize the true nature of the creative process, we learn that the exterior things are to be changed by a change of the interior spiritual attitude. Our spiritual attitude will always be determined by our conception of our relation to God or Infinite Spirit; and so when we begin to see that this relation is one of absolute reciprocity—that it is the self-recognition of Infinite Spirit from our own centre of consciousness—then we find that the whole Secret of Life consists in simple reliance upon the All-creating Spirit as consciously identifying itself with us. It has, so to say, awakened to a new mode of self-recognition peculiar to ourselves, in which we individually form the centre of its creative energy. To realize this is to specialize the Principle of Life. The logic of it is simple. We have found that the originating movement of Spirit from which all creation proceeds can only be Self-contemplation. Then, since the Original Spirit cannot change its nature its self-contemplation through our own minds must be as creative in, for, and through us as it ever was in the beginning; and consequently we find the original creative process repeated in ourselves and directed by the conscious thought of our own minds.

In all this there is no place for the consideration

of outward conditions, whether of body or circumstances; for they are only effects and not the cause; and therefore when we reach this stand-point we cease to take them into our calculations. Instead we employ the method of self-contemplation, knowing that this is the creative method, and so we contemplate ourselves as allied to the infinite Love and Wisdom of the Divine Spirit which will take form through our conscious thought, and so act creatively as a Special Providence entirely devoted to guarding, guiding, providing for, and illuminating us. The whole thing is perfectly natural when seen from a clear recognition of what the creative working of Spirit must be in itself; and when it is realized in this perfectly natural manner all strain and effort to compel its action ceases—we are at one with the All-creating Power which has now found a new centre in ourselves from which to continue its creative work to more perfect manifestation than could be attained through the unspecialized generic conditions of the merely cosmic order.

Now this is what Messiah stands for, and therefore it is written that " to them gave He power to become sons of God, even to as many as believe on His Name." This " belief " is the recognition of a universal principle and personal reliance upon it as a law which cannot be broken; for it is the Law of the whole creative process specialized in our own individuality. Then, too, however great may be the mystery, the removal and cleansing away of all sin follows as an essential part of this realization of new life; and it is in this sense that we may read all that the Bible tells us on this aspect of the subject. The *principle* of it is Love; for when we are reunited to the Parent Spirit in mutual confidence and love, what room is there on either side for any remembrance of our past failures?

This, then, is what Messiah stands for to the individual; but if we can conceive a nation based upon such a recognition of its special relation to the Directing Power of the Universe, such a people must of necessity become the leader of the nations, and those who oppose it must fail by a self-destructive principle inherent in the very nature of the position they take up. The leadership resulting from such a national self-recognition, will not be based upon conquest and compulsion, but will come naturally. Other nations will enquire the reason for the phenomenal success and prosperity of the favoured people, and finding this reason in a universal Law, they will begin to apply the same law in the same manner, and thus the same results will spread from country to country until at last the whole earth will be full of the glory of the Lord. And such a nation, and rather company of nations, exists. To trace its present development from its ancient beginnings is far beyond the scope of this volume, and still more to speculate upon its further growth; but to my readers on both sides of the Atlantic I may say that this people is the Anglo-Saxon race throughout the world. I write these lines upon the historic Hill of Tara; this will convey a hint to many of my readers. At some future time I may enlarge upon this subject; but at present my aim is merely to suggest some lines of thought arising from the Master's saying that " Salvation is of the Jews."

BIBLE MYSTERY AND BIBLE MEANING

Revised and Enlarged American Edition

A clear and logical interpretation of Bible truth, from the standpoint of modern metaphysics. Judge Troward starts with the supposition that the statements in the Bible are literally true, and from this point develops the thesis that the Book is not "a mere collection of world old fables or unintelligible dogmas, but a statement of great universal laws, all of which proceed simply and logically from the initial truth that creation is a process of evolution."

"Discloses himself a master thinker of new thought and a master of English in the expression of what he thinks."—*Stuart Law in the Ohio State Journal*.

Cloth, $1.50 Net - - - Postage, 10 cents

THE CREATIVE PROCESS IN THE INDIVIDUAL

The author says: "In the present volume I have endeavored to set before the reader the conception of a sequence of creative action, commencing with the formation of the globe and culminating in a vista of infinite possibilities attainable by every one who follows up the right line for their enfoldment . . . . . and if our speculation lead us to the conclusion that we have reached a point where we are not only able, but also required, by the law of our own being, to take a more active part in our personal evolution than heretofore, this discovery will afford us a new outlook upon life and widen our horizon with fresh interests and brightening hopes."

"It is a book that will greatly interest all who are interested in New Thought."—*Springfield (Mass.) Union.*

"In the advancement of his argument Mr. Troward bases his conclusions on scientific facts known and proved. . . . Above all his book is a study for the thinker."—*Salt Lake Tribune.*

"The book will repay study by the inspiration it holds for the philosophic reader."—*San Francisco Chronicle.*

Cloth, $1.25 - - - - Postage, 10 cents

THE DORÉ LECTURES ON MENTAL SCIENCE

Judge Troward supplemented his line of reasoning in the "Edinburgh Lectures on Mental Science," by a new series of lectures, published under the above title, deriving their name from the Doré Gallery in London, where the lectures were delivered. While his second volume in itself is scarcely a complete interpretation of Mental Science, it is a valuable addendum to his Edinburgh Lectures, the two volumes making plain to the seeker, by logical and scientific reasoning, the wonderful truth that while we are individuals, yet we are "one with the Father," and possess remarkable power in ourselves that has hitherto been overlooked.

This book was recently warmly commended in a discourse at Westminster Abbey by Archdeacon Wilberforce, who advised his hearers to read the work. The chapters are: "Entering Into the Spirit of It," "Individuality," "The New Thought and the New Order," "The Life of the Spirit," "Alpha and Omega," "The Creative Power of Thought," "The Great Affirmative," "Christ the Fulfilling of the Law," "The Story of Eden," "The Worship of Ishi," "The Shepherd and the Stone," "Salvation is of the Jews."

$1.00 Net - - - - - Postage, 10 cents